LEVEL 1 2

i-Scream edu

영어 공부의 핵심은 단어입니다.

케찹보카로
영어 단어 실력을 키우고,
상위 1% 어휘력을
따라잡아 보세요!

케찹보카 친구들

만화 스토리
친구들의 좌충우돌 일상이 그려진
재미있는 만화를 보며
단어 뜻을 배우고,
문장에 어떻게 활용되는지
알아볼 수 있어요!

Dennis	엉뚱하고 낙천적인 성격의 자유로운 영혼! 예측 불가에, 공부에도 관심이 없지만, 운이 좋아 뭘 해도 잘 풀린대요.	
Rod	인내심이 크고 생각도 깊은, 다정다감 엄친아! 개구쟁이 쌍둥이 누나, 애완묘 루나가 있어 혼자 있는 것보단 함께 하는 것을 좋아해요.	
Kiara	노래를 좋아하는 사교성의 아이콘! 솔직하고 모든 일에 적극적이지만, 금방 사랑에 빠지는 짝사랑 전문가래요.	
Sally	논리적이고 긍정적인 모범생! 친구들과 장난도 많이 치지만, 호기심이 많아 관심 분야에 다양한 지식을 갖고 있어요.	
Mong	친구들이 궁금한 것이 있을 때 나타나는 해결사! 너무 아는 것이 많아서 어느 별에서 왔는지 궁금하기도 해요.	

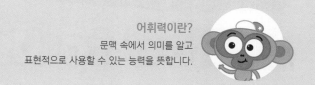

Know   **E**xercise   **T**hink   **C**heck   **H**abit

KETCH UP

망각 제로 단어 기억하기 습관으로
기억 장기화

게임으로 즐겁게 리뷰하고 테스트로 더블 체크

만화 스토리 〉 단어 〉 문장 순으로
단어 의미를 이해하며 모국어처럼 습득

이미지 연상 쓰기 연습으로 실제 단어 활용, 적용

주제별로 초등 필수＆고난도 단어 학습하며
상위 1% 단어 마스터

KETCH UP
Makes you Catch up.

체계적인 4 Steps 시스템으로 학습 완성!

Step 1	Step 2	Step 3	Step 4

Day 1~4

Day 5

Step 1

Warm up 망각 제로 & 스토리 단어 이해로 학습 준비하기

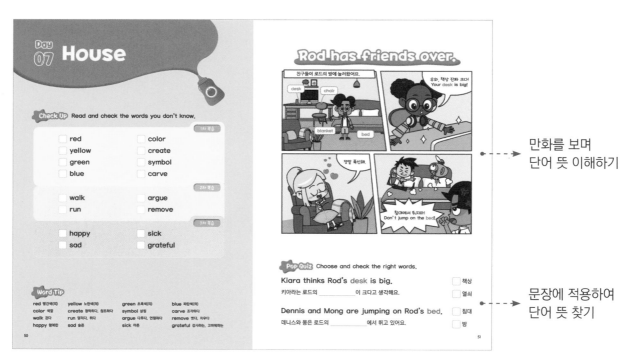

만화를 보며
단어 뜻 이해하기

문장에 적용하여
단어 뜻 찾기

※ 망각 제로는 p10에서 확인하세요!

Catch up 듣고, 말하고, 읽고, 쓰며, 상위 1% 단어 따라잡기

QR 찍어 단어 듣고 따라 말하기 ▶ 케찹병을 색칠하며 3번 반복하기

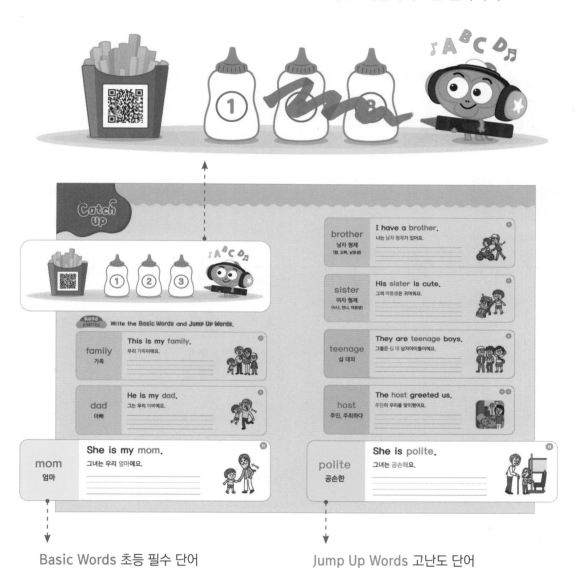

Basic Words 초등 필수 단어

Jump Up Words 고난도 단어

품사 기호

v	verb (동사)	**adv**	adverb (부사)	**conj**	conjunction (접속사)
n	noun (명사)	**prep**	preposition (전치사)	**pron**	pronoun (대명사)
a	adjective (형용사)	**det**	determiner (한정사)	**num**	numeral (수사)

케찹보카와 함께
상위 1% CATCH UP!

Step 3

Skill up 두뇌 자극 이미지 연상 학습으로 실력 강화하기

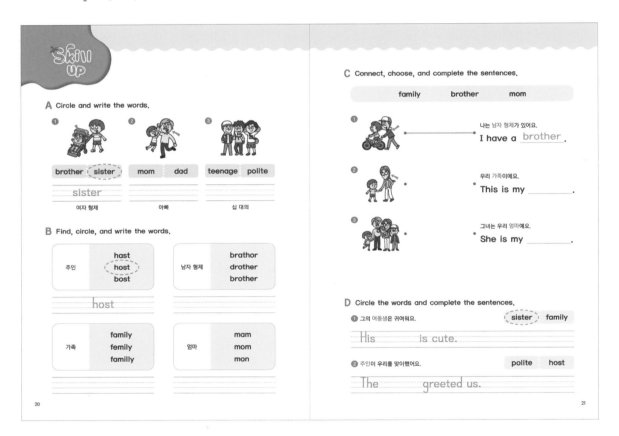

Wrap up 게임과 최종 평가를 통해 단어 학습 마무리하기

쉬어가기

다양한 유형의 재미있는 게임하며 단어 복습하기!

Word Maze
알맞은 스펠링으로 이뤄진
단어를 따라가
미로 찾기

Word Coloring
알맞은 단어를
색칠하며,
배운 단어 기억하기

Word Puzzle
주어진 문장에
알맞은 단어를 쓰며
퍼즐 완성하기

Word Search
다양한 알파벳 속
배운 단어를 찾아
쓰기 연습하기

복습&테스트

지금까지 배운 단어 정리하고, 테스트로 최종 점검!
뜯어서 쓰는 나만의 단어장까지!

Study Planner & Contents

Part 1

FINISH

START

망각 제로란?

> 망각 제로는
> 학습 주기를 활용해서 복습하는 거야.

> 지난번에 공부했던 단어 중에
> 아는 것과 모르는 것을 확인해 볼 수 있겠네!

Day 07 House

Check Up Read and check the words you don't know.

1차 복습

- [ ] red
- [ ] yellow
- [ ] green
- [ ] blue
- [ ] color
- [ ] create
- [ ] symbol
- [ ] carve

2차 복습

- [ ] walk
- [ ] run
- [ ] argue
- [ ] remove

3차 복습

- [ ] happy
- [ ] sad
- [ ] sick
- [ ] grateful

Word Tip

red 빨간색(의)   yellow 노란색(의)   green 초록색(의)   blue 파란색(의)
색   create 창작하다, 창조하다   symbol 상징   carve 조각하다
k 걷다   run 달리다, 뛰다   argue 다투다, 언쟁하다   remove 벗다, 치우다
happy   sad   sick   grateful 감사하는, 고마워하는

Check Up

복습 주기에 맞춰 반복 학습하기

1차 복습	1일 전 공부한 단어
2차 복습	3일 전 공부한 단어
3차 복습	7일 전 공부한 단어

Pop Quiz Choose and check the right words.

Kiara thinks Rod's desk is big.
키아라는 로드의 _____ 이 크다고 생각해요.
- [ ] 책상
- [ ] 열쇠

Dennis and Mong are jumping on Rod's bed.
데니스와 몽은 로드의 _____ 에서 뛰고 있어요.
- [ ] 침대
- [ ] 방

Word Tip

정확한 단어 뜻 확인하기

" 우리 같이
망각 제로 학습해 보자 "

※ 망각 제로는 [DAY 02]부터 시작합니다.

Let's make curry and rice!

Pop Quiz Choose and check the right words.

Sally brought potatoes.

샐리는 _____를 가져왔어요.

☑ 감자

☐ 당근

Dennis thinks it'll be delicious if they add grapes.

데니스는 _____를 넣으면 맛있을 거라고 생각해요.

☐ 배

☐ 포도

Catch Up

Listen, say, and color.

Read & Write   Write the **Basic Words** and **Jump Up Words**.

grape 포도	**These grapes are sweet.** ⁿ 이 포도들은 달콤해요. grape

potato 감자	**Try this baked potato.** ⁿ 이 구운 감자를 먹어 보세요. 

carrot 당근	**How many carrots do we need?** ⁿ 당근이 몇 개 필요한가요? 

pear
배

The pear is big.
그 배는 커요.

_____

apple
사과

I like apples.
나는 사과를 좋아해요.

_____

select
고르다, 선택하다

I selected some ripe bananas.
나는 잘 익은 바나나를 골랐어요.

_____

squeeze
짜내다, 압착하다

He squeezed the oranges.
그는 오렌지를 짜냈어요.

_____

piece
한 조각

She cut the apple into three pieces.
그녀는 사과를 세 조각으로 잘랐어요.

_____

A Circle and write the words.

①

grape | apple

grape

포도

②

potato | pear

배

③

carrot | potato

당근

B Connect and write the words.

① select

② squeeze

③ piece

④ apple

짜내다, 압착하다

고르다, 선택하다

사과

한 조각

select

C Connect, choose and complete the sentences.

selected	squeezed	potato

1

나는 잘 익은 바나나를 골랐어요.

I _____ some ripe bananas.

2

이 구운 감자를 먹어 보세요.

Try this baked _potato_.

3

그는 오렌지를 짜냈어요.

He _____ the oranges.

D Choose and complete the sentences.

pieces	carrots	grapes

1 이 포도들은 달콤해요.

These _grapes_ are sweet.

2 당근이 몇 개 필요한가요?

How many _____ do we need?

3 그녀는 사과를 세 조각으로 잘랐어요.

She cut the apple into three _____.

Check Up Read and check the words you don't know.

☐ grape   ☐ apple

☐ potato   ☐ select

☐ carrot   ☐ squeeze

☐ pear   ☐ piece

※ **망각 제로!** 1일 전 학습한 단어를 복습해요.

Word Tip

| grape 포도 | potato 감자 | carrot 당근 | pear 배 |
| apple 사과 | select 고르다, 선택하다 | squeeze 짜내다, 압착하다 | piece 한 조각 |

Happy birthday!

Pop Quiz Choose and check the right words.

There are many gifts.

_____ 이 많이 있어요.

☐ 선물
☐ 공포

Kiara and her friends should blow up all the balloons.

키아라와 친구들은 _____ 을 모두 불어야 해요.

☐ 장난감
☐ 풍선

 Listen, say, and color.

 Write the **Basic Words** and **Jump Up Words**.

ball 공	**There are many kinds of** balls. 많은 종류의 공들이 있어요.

bat 방망이, 배트	**I hit the ball with a** bat. 나는 방망이로 공을 쳤어요.

balloon 풍선	**We blew up the** balloons. 우리는 풍선을 불었어요.

gift
선물

My gift is a robot. (n)

내 선물은 로봇이에요.

---

toy
장난감

She is playing with her toys. (n)

그녀는 장난감을 가지고 놀고 있어요.

---

burst
터뜨리다, 터지다

He burst the balloon. (v)

그가 풍선을 터뜨렸어요.

---

fear
공포, 두려움

I have a fear of ladders. (n)

나는 사다리에 대한 공포가 있어요.

---

rule
규칙

I know the rules of the game. (n)

나는 게임의 규칙을 알아요.

A Circle the letters and complete the words.

1 a (u) i (e)

r u l e
규칙

2 f b z r

e a _
공포, 두려움

3 f k r u

b _ s t
터뜨리다, 터지다

B Unscramble and write the words.

1 공   a l b l   ball

2 선물   i f t g

3 장난감   y o t

4 풍선   l a l b o o n

C Connect, choose, and complete the sentences.

balloons	toys	balls

1

우리는 풍선을 불었어요.

We blew up the _____.

2

많은 종류의 공들이 있어요.

There are many kinds of _____.

3

그녀는 장난감을 가지고 놀고 있어요.

She is playing with her _____.

D Circle the words and complete the sentences.

1 내 선물은 로봇이에요.   (gift)   toy

My _____ is a robot.

2 나는 방망이로 공을 쳤어요.   ball   bat

I hit the ball with a _____.

Day 03 Food Preparation

Check Up Read and check the words you don't know.

1차 복습

☐ ball	☐ toy
☐ bat	☐ burst
☐ balloon	☐ fear
☐ gift	☐ rule

※ **망각 제로!** 1일 전 학습한 단어를 복습해요.

ball 공

bat 방망이, 배트

balloon 풍선

gift 선물

toy 장난감

burst 터뜨리다, 터지다

fear 공포, 두려움

rule 규칙

What a delicious dinner!

Rod and his family eat dinner together.

로드와 그의 가족은 함께 저녁을 _____.

☐ 붓다

☐ 먹다

Rod thinks the food tastes good.

로드는 음식 _____ 좋다고 생각해요.

☐ 맛이 ~하다

☐ 끓이다

Listen & Say

Listen, say, and color.

Read & Write

Write the Basic Words and Jump Up Words.

knife 칼, 나이프	**The knife is sharp.** 그 칼은 날카로워요. _____

dish 접시, 요리	**I washed the dishes.** 나는 접시들을 설거지했어요. _____

spoon 숟가락	**I need a spoon.** 나는 숟가락이 필요해요. _____

eat
먹다

I like to eat carrots. Ⓥ

나는 당근 먹는 것을 좋아해요.

taste
맛이 ~하다, 맛

It tastes good. Ⓥ Ⓝ

맛이 좋아요.

refrigerator
냉장고

Put the food in the refrigerator. Ⓝ

그 음식을 냉장고에 넣으세요.

pour
붓다, 따르다

I poured some milk into my cereal. Ⓥ

나는 시리얼에 우유를 부었어요.

boil
끓이다, 끓다

I boiled some water. Ⓥ

나는 물을 끓였어요.

Skill UP

A Circle and write the words.

1 eat : pour

_____

붓다, 따르다

2 dish : spoon

_____

접시

3 boil : taste

_____

맛이 ~하다, 맛

B Find, circle, and write the words.

숟가락	spuon
	spoun
	(spoon)

spoon

칼	naife
	knife
	knaif

_____

끓이다, 끓다	poil
	boul
	boil

_____

냉장고	refrigerator
	refrigerater
	refregirator

_____

C Connect and fill in the blanks.

1

2

3

The knife is sharp.

그 ____칼____ 은 날카로워요.

I need a spoon.

나는 _____이 필요해요.

I like to eat carrots.

나는 당근 _____ 것을 좋아해요.

D Choose and complete the sentences.

tastes	dishes	boiled

1 나는 접시들을 설거지했어요.

I washed the _____.

2 나는 물을 약간 끓였어요.

I _____ some water.

3 맛이 좋아요.

It _____ good.

Check Up Read and check the words you don't know.

1차 복습

- [ ] knife
- [ ] dish
- [ ] spoon
- [ ] eat

- [ ] taste
- [ ] refrigerator
- [ ] pour
- [ ] boil

2차 복습

- [ ] grape
- [ ] potato

- [ ] squeeze
- [ ] piece

※ **망각 제로!** 1일 전 3일 전 학습한 단어를 복습해요.

Word Tip

knife 칼, 나이프	**dish** 접시, 요리	**spoon** 숟가락	**eat** 먹다
taste 맛이 ~하다, 맛	**refrigerator** 냉장고	**pour** 붓다, 따르다	**boil** 끓이다, 끓다
grape 포도	**potato** 감자	**squeeze** 짜내다, 압착하다	**piece** 한 조각

It's hot today.

Pop Quiz Choose and check the right words.

Dennis suggests drinking something cool.

데니스는 뭔가 시원한 것을 _____ 제안해요.

- [ ] 보다
- [ ] 마시다

Mong suggests watching a movie.

몽은 _____를 보자고 제안해요.

- [ ] 우산
- [ ] 영화

29

 **Listen, say, and color.**

 Write the **Basic Words** and **Jump Up Words**.

umbrella 우산	**Take my umbrella.** 내 우산을 가져가세요. _____

n

fan 선풍기, 부채	**The fan is on the table.** 선풍기가 탁자 위에 있어요. _____

n

watch 보다	**I'm watching TV.** 나는 TV를 보고 있어요. _____

v

movie
영화

Let's watch a movie **in my room.** (n)

내 방에서 영화를 보자.

_____

- - - - - - - - - - - - - - - - - - - -

_____

drink
마시다

We drink **water.** (v)

우리는 물을 마셔요.

_____

- - - - - - - - - - - - - - - - - - - -

_____

whole
전체의

He ate the whole **cake.** (a)

그는 케이크를 통째로 먹었어요.

_____

- - - - - - - - - - - - - - - - - - - -

_____

skip
생략하다,
건너뛰다

I will skip **dessert tonight.** (v)

나는 오늘 밤 디저트는 생략할게요.

_____

- - - - - - - - - - - - - - - - - - - -

_____

mood
기분

He's in a good mood **today.** (n)

그는 오늘 기분이 좋아요.

_____

- - - - - - - - - - - - - - - - - - - -

_____

A Circle and trace the words.

기분	선풍기	영화	우산	건너뛰다	마시다

fan   umbrella   drink

B Unscramble and write the words.

1 기분   d o m o

2 영화   m v i e o

3 생략하다,
건너뛰다   k i p s

4 전체의   h o w l e

C Connect and fill in the blanks.

1.

Let's watch a movie in my room.

내 방에서 _____를 보자.

2.

He's in a good mood today.

그는 오늘 _____이 좋아요.

3.

He ate the whole cake.

그는 케이크를 _____ 먹었어요.

D Circle the words and complete the sentences.

1 선풍기가 탁자 위에 있어요.

umbrella	fan

The _____ is on the table.

2 나는 오늘 밤 디저트는 생략할게요.

skip	watch

I will _____ dessert tonight.

Day 05 Neighborhood

Check Up Read and check the words you don't know.

1차 복습

- [ ] umbrella
- [ ] fan
- [ ] watch
- [ ] movie
- [ ] drink
- [ ] whole
- [ ] skip
- [ ] mood

2차 복습

- [ ] ball
- [ ] bat
- [ ] fear
- [ ] rule

※**망각 제로!** 1일 전 3일 전 학습한 단어를 복습해요.

Word Tip

umbrella 우산	**fan** 선풍기, 부채	**watch** 보다	**movie** 영화
drink 마시다	**whole** 전체의	**skip** 생략하다, 건너뛰다	**mood** 기분
ball 공	**bat** 방망이, 배트	**fear** 공포, 두려움	**rule** 규칙

Welcome to my neighborhood.

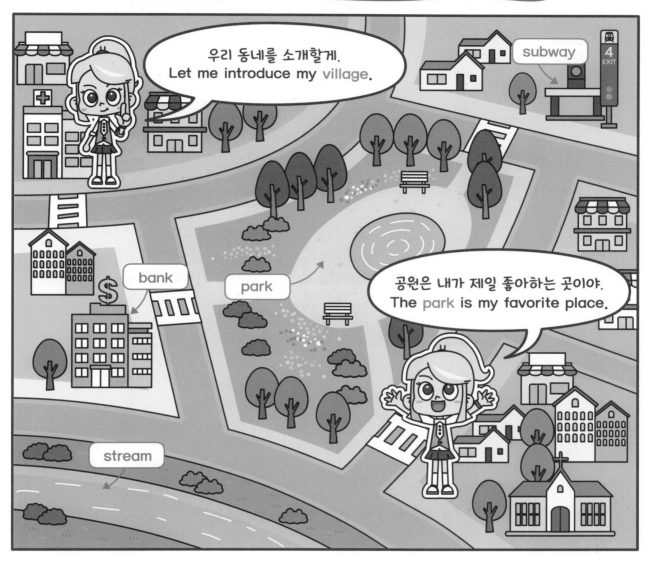

Pop Quiz Choose and check the right words.

Sally is introducing her village.

샐리는 자신의 _____을 소개하고 있어요.

The park is Sally's favorite place.

_____은 샐리가 가장 좋아하는 장소예요.

- [ ] 농장
- [ ] 마을
- [ ] 공원
- [ ] 은행

Catch Up

Listen & Say Listen, say, and color.

Read & Write Write the Basic Words and Jump Up Words.

park 공원	**Let's meet at the park.** 공원에서 만나자. _____ _____ _____ 

bank 은행	**He works at the bank.** 그는 은행에서 일해요. _____ _____ _____ 

subway 지하철	**They are on the subway.** 그들은 지하철을 탔어요. _____ _____ _____ 

farm
농장

They grow wheat on the farm. (n)

그들은 농장에서 밀을 키워요.

think
생각하다

Let's think about helping our neighbors. (v)

이웃을 돕는 것에 대해 생각해 보자.

village
마을, 촌락

We live in a small village. (n)

우리는 작은 마을에 살아요.

stream
개울, 시내

We crossed a stream. (n)

우리는 개울을 건넜어요.

neighbor
이웃

They are my neighbors. (n)

그들은 나의 이웃이에요.

A Circle the letters and complete the words.

1

p　f　n　m

_ a r
농장

2

f　t　y　h

_ _ i n k
생각하다

3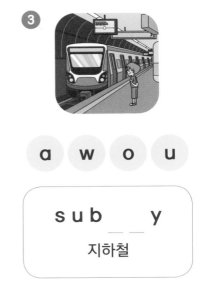

a　w　o　u

s u b _ _ y
지하철

B Connect and write the words.

1 neighbor　•　　•　마을, 촌락

2 stream　•　　•　개울, 시내

3 village　•　　•　이웃

4 park　•　　•　공원

C Connect, choose, and complete the sentences.

bank	subway	village

1

그는 은행에서 일해요.

He works at the _____.

2

우리는 작은 마을에 살아요.

We live in a small _____.

3

그들은 지하철을 탔어요.

They are on the _____.

D Circle the words and complete the sentences.

1 우리는 개울을 건넜어요.

subway   stream

We crossed a _____.

2 공원에서 만나자.

park   bank

Let's meet at the _____.

FRUITS

START

grape

poteto

baell

potato

mobie

gifte

ball

spoon

movie

farm

knife

park

pear

parkk

knife

nife

carrot

gift

balel

farme

FINISH

Farmers market

40

grape 포도	**potato** 감자	**carrot** 당근	**pear** 배	**apple** 사과

select 고르다, 선택하다	**squeeze** 짜내다, 압착하다	**piece** 한 조각	**ball** 공	**bat** 방망이, 배트

balloon 풍선	**gift** 선물	**toy** 장난감	**burst** 터뜨리다, 터지다	**fear** 공포, 두려움

rule 규칙	**knife** 칼, 나이프	**dish** 접시, 요리	**spoon** 숟가락	**eat** 먹다

taste 맛이 ~하다, 맛	**refrigerator** 냉장고	**pour** 붓다, 따르다	**boil** 끓이다, 끓다	**umbrella** 우산

fan 선풍기, 부채	**watch** 보다	**movie** 영화	**drink** 마시다	**whole** 전체의

skip 생략하다, 건너뛰다	**mood** 기분	**park** 공원	**bank** 은행	**subway** 지하철

farm 농장	**think** 생각하다	**village** 마을, 촌락	**stream** 개울, 시내	**neighbor** 이웃

❶ grape		㉑ 당근	
❷ potato		㉒ 배	
❸ apple		㉓ 짜내다, 압착하다	
❹ select		㉔ 한 조각	
❺ ball		㉕ 풍선	
❻ bat		㉖ 선물	
❼ toy		㉗ 공포, 두려움	
❽ burst		㉘ 규칙	
❾ knife		㉙ 숟가락	
❿ dish		㉚ 먹다	
⓫ taste		㉛ 붓다, 따르다	
⓬ refrigerator		㉜ 끓이다, 끓다	
⓭ umbrella		㉝ 보다	
⓮ fan		㉞ 영화	
⓯ drink		㉟ 생략하다, 건너뛰다	
⓰ whole		㊱ 기분	
⓱ park		㊲ 지하철	
⓲ bank		㊳ 농장	
⓳ think		㊴ 개울, 시내	
⓴ village		㊵ 이웃	

Part 2

FINISH

START

Day 06 Personality

Check Up Read and check the words you don't know.

1차 복습

☐ park ☐ think

☐ bank ☐ village

☐ subway ☐ stream

☐ farm ☐ neighbor

2차 복습

☐ knife ☐ pour

☐ dish ☐ boil

※**망각 제로!** 1일 전 3일 전 학습한 단어를 복습해요.

Word Tip

park 공원   **bank** 은행   **subway** 지하철   **farm** 농장
think 생각하다   **village** 마을, 촌락   **stream** 개울, 시내   **neighbor** 이웃
knife 칼, 나이프   **dish** 접시, 요리   **pour** 붓다, 따르다   **boil** 끓이다, 끓다

Pick me!

Pop Quiz Choose and check the right words.

Rod is kind to everyone.

로드는 모두에게 ＿＿＿＿＿＿＿.

☐ 친절한
☐ 현명한

Kiara is brave.

키아라는 ＿＿＿＿＿＿＿.

☐ 용감한
☐ 온화한

Read & Write Write the **Basic Words** and **Jump Up Words**.

nice 좋은, 멋진	**He is a nice man.** ⓐ 그는 좋은 사람이에요. _____
kind 친절한	**She is kind.** ⓐ 그녀는 친절해요. _____
brave 용감한	**We are brave.** ⓐ 우리는 용감해요. _____

like
좋아하다

I like my friends. ⓥ

나는 내 친구들을 좋아해요.

_____

_____

worry
걱정하다

I worry a lot. ⓥ

나는 걱정을 많이 해요.

_____

_____

gentle
다정한, 온화한

She is gentle with her kids. ⓐ

그녀는 아이들에게 다정해요.

_____

_____

wise
현명한,
지혜로운

There was a wise old man. ⓐ

현명한 노인이 있었어요.

_____

_____

silly
어리석은,
바보 같은

Don't be silly. ⓐ

어리석은 행동 하지 말아요.

_____

_____

Skill UP

A Circle and trace the words.

①
| 어리석은 | 좋은 |

nice

②
| 걱정하다 | 좋아하다 |

worry

③
| 용감한 | 다정한 |

gentle

B Find, circle, and write the words.

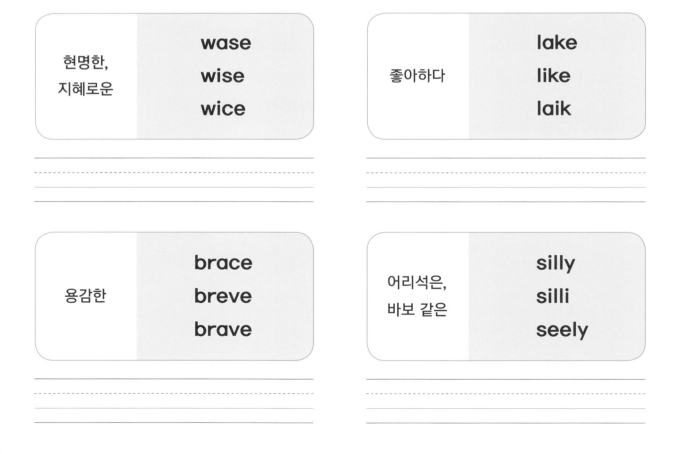

| 현명한, 지혜로운 | wase
wise
wice |

| 좋아하다 | lake
like
laik |

| 용감한 | brace
breve
brave |

| 어리석은,
바보 같은 | silly
silli
seely |

48

C Connect and fill in the blanks.

1.

She is kind.

그녀는 _____요.

2.

I like my friends.

나는 내 친구들을 _____.

3.

There was a wise old man.

_____ 노인이 있었어요.

D Choose and complete the sentences.

brave   silly   worry

1 나는 걱정을 많이 해요.

I _____ a lot.

2 어리석은 행동하지 말아요.

Don't be _____.

3 우리는 용감해요.

We are _____.

Day 07 Movements

Check UP Read and check the words you don't know.

- [ ] nice
- [ ] kind
- [ ] brave
- [ ] like

- [ ] worry
- [ ] gentle
- [ ] wise
- [ ] silly

- [ ] umbrella
- [ ] fan

- [ ] skip
- [ ] mood

- [ ] carrot
- [ ] pear

- [ ] apple
- [ ] select

※ 망각 제로! 1일 전 3일 전 7일 전 학습한 단어를 복습해요.

 **Word Tip**

nice 좋은, 멋진	**kind** 친절한	**brave** 용감한	**like** 좋아하다
worry 걱정하다	**gentle** 다정한, 온화한	**wise** 현명한, 지혜로운	**silly** 어리석은, 바보 같은
umbrella 우산	**fan** 선풍기, 부채	**skip** 생략하다, 건너뛰다	**mood** 기분
carrot 당근	**pear** 배	**apple** 사과	**select** 고르다, 선택하다

Cats can leap very high.

Pop Quiz Choose and check the right words.

Rod made a cat tower last weekend.

로드는 지난 주말에 캣 타워를 _____.

☐ 말하다

☐ 만들다

Kiara is worried if Luna could fall off.

키아라는 루나가 _____까 봐 걱정해요.

☐ 잡다

☐ 떨어지다

51

 Listen, say, and color.

 Write the Basic Words and Jump Up Words.

make 만들다	**Let's make a robot.** 로봇을 만들자.

fall 떨어지다	**Don't fall off the chair.** 의자에서 떨어지지 않도록 해.

say 말하다	**I say, "Hello."** 나는 "안녕."이라고 말해요.

Hello!

show
보여 주다, 공연

I show **Mom my prize.** (v)(n)

나는 엄마에게 내 상을 보여 줘요.

_____

catch
잡다

Catch the ball, please. (v)

공을 잡으세요.

_____

journey
여행

We are going on a journey**.** (n)

우리는 여행을 가요.

_____

leap
뛰다, 뛰어오르다

Monkeys leap **from tree to tree.** (v)

원숭이가 나무에서 나무로 뛰어다녀요.

_____

seek
찾다, 구하다

Dad is seeking **his daughter.** (v)

아빠가 딸을 찾고 있어요.

_____

Skill Up

A Circle the letters and complete the words.

1

a e i o

m _ k _
만들다

2

f c s h

c a t _ _
잡다

3

e a i e

s _ _ k
찾다, 구하다

B Connect and write the words.

1 leap •   • 여행   _____

2 journey •   • 떨어지다   _____

3 fall •   • 말하다   _____

4 say •   • 뛰다, 뛰어오르다 _____

C Connect, choose, and complete the sentences.

| leap | show | journey |

1 우리는 여행을 가요.

We are going on a _____.

2 원숭이가 나무에서 나무로 뛰어다녀요.

Monkeys _____ from tree to tree.

3 나는 엄마에게 내 상을 보여 줘요.

I _____ Mom my prize.

D Circle the words and complete the sentences.

1 의자에서 떨어지지 않도록 해.

fall : seek

Don't _____ off the chair.

2 공을 잡으세요.

Leap : Catch

_____ the ball, please.

Day 08 Transportation

Check Up Read and check the words you don't know.

1차 복습

☐ make   ☐ catch
☐ fall   ☐ journey
☐ say   ☐ leap
☐ show   ☐ seek

2차 복습

☐ park   ☐ stream
☐ bank   ☐ neighbor

3차 복습

☐ balloon   ☐ toy
☐ gift   ☐ burst

※ 망각 제로! 1일 전 3일 전 7일 전 학습한 단어를 복습해요.

Word Tip

make 만들다   fall 떨어지다   say 말하다   show 보여 주다, 공연
catch 잡다   journey 여행   leap 뛰다, 뛰어오르다   seek 찾다, 구하다
park 공원   bank 은행   stream 개울, 시내   neighbor 이웃
balloon 풍선   gift 선물   toy 장난감   burst 터뜨리다, 터지다

What kind of transportation do you like?

Pop Quiz Choose and check the right words.

Sally likes to take a train.

샐리는 _____ 타는 것을 좋아해요.

Mong says the airplane is the fastest.

몽은 _____가 가장 빠르다고 말해요.

☐ 배

☐ 기차

☐ 자동차

☐ 비행기

Listen, say, and color.

Read & Write

Write the **Basic Words** and **Jump Up Words**.

car 자동차	**I drive a car.** 나는 자동차를 운전해요.

train 기차	**Let's take the train.** 기차를 타자.

airplane 비행기	**An airplane is flying in the sky.** 비행기가 하늘을 날고 있어요.

boat
보트, (작은) 배

There's a boat on the river. [n]

강 위에 보트가 있어요.

_____

_____

ship
(큰) 배, 선박

I see a big ship. [n]

나는 큰 배를 봐요.

_____

_____

float
뜨다

Boats float on water. [v]

보트가 물 위에 떠 있어요.

_____

_____

passenger
승객

Some passengers got off the bus. [n]

승객 몇 명이 버스에서 내렸어요.

_____

_____

similar
비슷한

The two cars look similar. [a]

두 자동차는 비슷해 보여요.

_____

_____

A Circle and write the words.

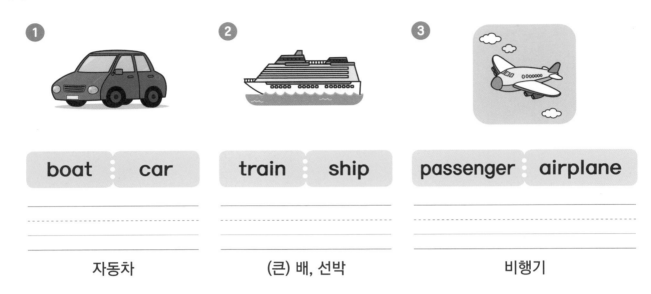

1

boat	car

_____

자동차

2

train	ship

_____

(큰) 배, 선박

3

passenger	airplane

_____

비행기

B Unscramble and write the words.

1 승객   s s p a e n g e r   _____

2 기차   a r t n i   _____

3 뜨다   l f t a o   _____

4 비슷한   i m s i l r a   _____

C Connect and fill in the blanks.

①

Boats float **on water.**

보트가 물 위에 _____.

②

Some passengers **got off the bus.**

_____ 몇 명이 버스에서 내렸어요.

③

Let's take the train**.**

_____를 타자.

D Choose and complete the sentences.

boat   similar   ship

① 강 위에 보트가 있어요.

There's a _____ on the river.

② 두 자동차는 비슷해 보여요.

The two cars look _____.

③ 나는 큰 배를 봐요.

I see a big _____.

Day 09 Reading

Check Up Read and check the words you don't know.

1차 복습

- car
- train
- airplane
- boat

- ship
- float
- passenger
- similar

2차 복습

- nice
- kind

- wise
- silly

3차 복습

- umbrella
- fan

- skip
- mood

※ 망각 제로! 1일 전 3일 전 7일 전 학습한 단어를 복습해요.

We are in the library.

Choose and check the right words.

Rod wants to read the journal.

로드는 _____를 읽고 싶어 해요.

☐ 소설
☐ 잡지

Kiara knows the book that Sally has.

키아라는 샐리가 가지고 있는 책을 _____.

☐ 알다
☐ 쓰다

Read &Write Write the **Basic Words** and **Jump Up Words**.

read 읽다	**I read before bed.** ^v 나는 자기 전에 책을 읽어요.

book 책	**This is a book.** ⁿ 이것은 책이에요.

know 알다	**Now I know how the story ends.** ^v 이제 나는 이야기의 결말을 알아요.

write
쓰다

I like to write. v

나는 글을 쓰는 것을 좋아해요.

name
이름

I know the name of the writer. n

나는 그 작가의 이름을 알아요.

novel
소설

The novels are interesting. n

그 소설은 흥미진진해요.

poem
시

She read a poem. n

그녀는 시를 읽었어요.

journal
잡지, 신문

I read it in a scientific journal. n

나는 그것을 과학 잡지에서 읽었어요.

A Circle the letters and complete the words.

①

a   o   u   o

b _ k
책

②

l   w   a   r

_ _ i t e
쓰다

③

a   e   i   u

n _ m _
이름

B Connect and write the words.

① novel •   • 잡지, 신문 ————————

② journal •   • 시 ————————

③ poem •   • 알다 ————————

④ know •   • 소설 ————————

C Connect, choose, and complete the sentences.

| read | journal | novels |

1

나는 자기 전에 책을 읽어요.

I _____ before bed.

2

그 소설은 흥미진진해요.

The _____ are interesting.

3

나는 그것을 과학 잡지에서 읽었어요.

I read it in a scientific _____.

D Circle the words and complete the sentences.

1 그녀는 시를 읽었어요.

| poem | name |

She read a _____.

2 나는 글을 쓰는 것을 좋아해요.

| write | know |

I like to _____.

Day 10 School

Check Up Read and check the words you don't know.

1차 복습

☐ read   ☐ name
☐ book   ☐ novel
☐ know   ☐ poem
☐ write   ☐ journal

2차 복습

☐ make   ☐ leap
☐ fall   ☐ seek

3차 복습

☐ watch   ☐ drink
☐ movie   ☐ whole

※ **망각 제로!** 1일 전 3일 전 7일 전 학습한 단어를 복습해요.

Word Tip

read 읽다	book 책	know 알다	write 쓰다
name 이름	novel 소설	poem 시	journal 잡지, 신문
make 만들다	fall 떨어지다	leap 뛰다, 뛰어오르다	seek 찾다, 구하다
watch 보다	movie 영화	drink 마시다	whole 전체의

Role-playing is fun!

Pop Quiz Choose and check the right words.

Mong is teaching English.

몽은 영어를 ＿＿＿＿＿＿ 있어요.

☐ 가르치다

☐ 존경하다

Rod and Sally are studying hard.

로드와 샐리는 열심히 ＿＿＿＿＿＿ 있어요.

☐ 말하다

☐ 공부하다

Listen, say, and color.

Read &Write

Write the **Basic Words** and **Jump Up Words**.

teach 가르치다	**I teach English.** 나는 영어를 가르쳐요. 
study 공부하다	**I study English.** 나는 영어를 공부해요.
teacher 선생님	**He is my teacher.** 그분은 제 선생님이에요. 

student
학생

She is a student. n

그녀는 학생이에요.

---

school
학교

This is my school. n

이곳은 나의 학교예요.

classroom
교실

This is my classroom. n

이곳은 나의 교실이에요.

---

admire
존경하다

We admire our teacher. v

우리는 선생님을 존경해요.

---

task
일, 과제

My task is cleaning the whiteboard. n

내 일은 화이트보드를 청소하는 것이에요.

A Circle and trace the words.

1

선생님	학생

student

2

학교	교실

school

3

가르치다	공부하다

teach

B Unscramble and write the words.

1 선생님   a t e h c r e

2 공부하다   t s u d y

3 존경하다   d m i a r e

4 일, 과제   s t a k

C Connect and fill in the blanks.

1

He is my teacher.

그분은 제 _____ 이에요.

2

This is my classroom.

이곳은 나의 _____ 이에요.

3

My task **is cleaning the whiteboard.**

내 _____ 은 화이트보드를 청소하는 것이에요.

D Choose and complete the sentences.

admire   study   school

1 우리는 선생님을 존경해요.

We _____ our teacher.

2 이곳은 나의 학교예요.

This is my _____.

3 나는 영어를 공부해요.

I _____ English.

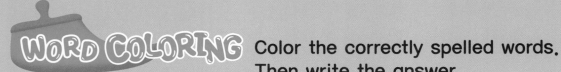

Q. What kind of transportation do you see?

nice 좋은, 멋진	**kind** 친절한	**brave** 용감한	**like** 좋아하다	**worry** 걱정하다
gentle 다정한, 온화한	**wise** 현명한, 지혜로운	**silly** 어리석은, 바보 같은	**make** 만들다	**fall** 떨어지다
say 말하다	**show** 보여 주다, 공연	**catch** 잡다	**journey** 여행	**leap** 뛰다, 뛰어오르다
seek 찾다, 구하다	**car** 자동차	**train** 기차	**airplane** 비행기	**boat** 보트, (작은) 배
ship (큰) 배, 선박	**float** 뜨다	**passenger** 승객	**similar** 비슷한	**read** 읽다
book 책	**know** 알다	**write** 쓰다	**name** 이름	**novel** 소설
poem 시	**journal** 잡지, 신문	**teach** 가르치다	**study** 공부하다	**teacher** 선생님
student 학생	**school** 학교	**classroom** 교실	**admire** 존경하다	**task** 일, 과제

Day 06~10

맞힌 개수 : ☐ / 40

❶ nice		**㉑ 용감한**	
❷ kind		**㉒ 좋아하다**	
❸ silly		**㉓ 현명한, 지혜로운**	
❹ gentle		**㉔ 걱정하다**	
❺ make		**㉕ 말하다**	
❻ fall		**㉖ 보여 주다, 공연**	
❼ catch		**㉗ 뛰다, 뛰어오르다**	
❽ journey		**㉘ 찾다, 구하다**	
❾ car		**㉙ 비행기**	
❿ train		**㉚ 보트, (작은) 배**	
⓫ ship		**㉛ 승객**	
⓬ float		**㉜ 비슷한**	
⓭ read		**㉝ 알다**	
⓮ book		**㉞ 쓰다**	
⓯ name		**㉟ 시**	
⓰ novel		**㊱ 잡지, 신문**	
⓱ teach		**㊲ 선생님**	
⓲ study		**㊳ 학생**	
⓳ school		**㊴ 존경하다**	
⓴ classroom		**㊵ 일, 과제**	

Part 3

FINISH

START

Check Up Read and check the words you don't know.

1차 복습

- [ ] teach
- [ ] study
- [ ] teacher
- [ ] student
- [ ] school
- [ ] classroom
- [ ] admire
- [ ] task

2차 복습

- [ ] car
- [ ] train
- [ ] passenger
- [ ] similar

3차 복습

- [ ] subway
- [ ] farm
- [ ] think
- [ ] village

※ 망각 제로! 1일 전 3일 전 7일 전 학습한 단어를 복습해요.

Word Tip

teach 가르치다	study 공부하다	teacher 선생님	student 학생
school 학교	classroom 교실	admire 존경하다	task 일, 과제
car 자동차	train 기차	passenger 승객	similar 비슷한
subway 지하철	farm 농장	think 생각하다	village 마을, 촌락

Sleep tight, Luna.

PopQuiz Choose and check the right words.

Rod will visit his grandfather.

로드는 할아버지 댁을 _____ 거예요.

- [ ] 방문하다
- [ ] 함께 하다

Rod's dad asks Rod if he has packed his bag.

로드의 아빠는 로드가 _____ 물어요.

- [ ] 짐을 싸다
- [ ] 경고하다

Listen, say, and color.

Write the **Basic Words** and **Jump Up Words**.

	I will visit my friend in Japan. ⓥ
visit 방문하다	나는 일본에 있는 친구 집을 방문할 거예요. _____ _____ 

	I will sleep in a tent. ⓥ
sleep 자다	나는 텐트 안에서 잘 거예요. _____ _____ 

	I switched on the lamp. ⓝ
lamp 램프, 등	나는 램프를 켰어요. _____ _____

join
함께 하다,
가입하다

Will you join me on this trip? (v)

이번 여행에 나와 함께 가주시겠어요?

_____
- -
_____

joy
기쁨, 즐거움

They jumped for joy. (n)

그들은 기쁨에 날뛰었어요.

_____
- -
_____

warn
경고하다,
주의를 주다

She warned me about the danger. (v)

그녀는 위험에 대해 경고했어요.

_____
- -
_____

pack
(짐을) 싸다,
꾸러미

We packed clothes for our trip. (v)(n)

우리는 여행을 위해 옷을 쌌어요.

_____
- -
_____

sense
감각

He has a good sense of direction. (n)

그는 방향 감각이 좋아요.

_____
- -
_____

A Circle and write the words.

1

visit	sleep

_____

자다

2

warn	join

_____

경고하다, 주의를 주다

3

pack	visit

_____

(짐을) 싸다, 꾸러미

B Connect and write the words.

1 visit •   • 함께 하다,
                     가입하다   _____

2 sense •   • 감각   _____

3 joy •   • 방문하다   _____

4 join •   • 기쁨, 즐거움   _____

C Connect, choose, and complete the sentences.

sense	visit	lamp

1 나는 램프를 켰어요.

I switched on the _____ .

2 그는 방향 감각이 좋아요.

He has a good _____ of direction.

3 나는 일본에 있는 친구 집을 방문할 거예요.

I will _____ my friend in Japan.

D Circle the words and complete the sentences.

1 나는 텐트 안에서 잘 거예요.

join	sleep

I will _____ in a tent.

2 그들은 기쁨에 날뛰었어요.

joy	sense

They jumped for _____ .

Day 12 School

Check Up Read and check the words you don't know.

1차 복습

- [ ] visit
- [ ] sleep
- [ ] lamp
- [ ] join
- [ ] joy
- [ ] warn
- [ ] pack
- [ ] sense

2차 복습

- [ ] read
- [ ] book
- [ ] poem
- [ ] journal

3차 복습

- [ ] brave
- [ ] worry
- [ ] like
- [ ] gentle

※ 망각 제로! 1일 전 3일 전 7일 전 학습한 단어를 복습해요.

 **Word Tip**

visit 방문하다	**sleep** 자다	**lamp** 램프, 등	**join** 함께 하다, 가입하다
joy 기쁨, 즐거움	**warn** 경고하다, 주의를 주다	**pack** (짐을) 싸다, 꾸러미	**sense** 감각
read 읽다	**book** 책	**poem** 시	**journal** 잡지, 신문
brave 용감한	**worry** 걱정하다	**like** 좋아하다	**gentle** 다정한, 온화한

84

Let's play rock, paper, scissors!

![Pop Quiz] **Choose and check the right words.**

Mong brought a basket full of candy.

몽은 사탕이 가득 든 _____를 가지고 왔어요.

☐ 바위

☐ 바구니

Kiara wants the star-shaped.

키아라는 별 _____을 원해요.

☐ 모양

☐ 종이

 Write the **Basic Words** and **Jump Up Words**.

scissors 가위	**I need scissors.**  나는 가위가 필요해요. _____ _____

paper 종이	**I need paper.**  나는 종이가 필요해요. _____ _____

rock 바위, 돌	**They sat on a rock.** 그들은 바위 위에 앉았어요. _____ _____

have
가지다

I have a pencil and some paper. ⓥ

나는 연필과 종이를 가지고 있어요.

---

basket
바구니

There are some balls in the basket. ⓝ

공 몇 개가 바구니 안에 있어요.

---

shape
모양

We draw shapes in the sand. ⓝ

우리는 모래에 모양을 그려요.

---

popular
인기 있는

He is popular at school. ⓐ

그는 학교에서 인기 있어요.

---

sure
확신하는

I'm sure it won't rain. ⓐ

나는 비가 오지 않을 거라고 확신해요.

A Circle and trace the words.

1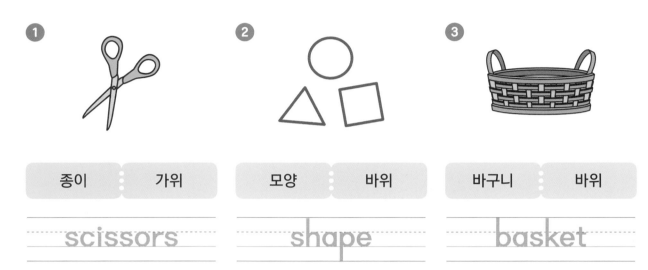

| 종이 | 가위 |

scissors

2

| 모양 | 바위 |

shape

3

| 바구니 | 바위 |

basket

B Unscramble and write the words.

1 종이   e p r p a

2 인기 있는   u p l o p a r

3 바위, 돌   o c r k

4 확신하는   u e s r

C Connect and fill in the blanks.

1

They sat on a rock.

그들은 ＿＿＿＿＿＿＿ 위에 앉았어요.

2

I need paper.

나는 ＿＿＿＿＿＿＿가 필요해요.

3

He is popular at school.

그는 학교에서 ＿＿＿＿＿＿＿요.

D Choose and complete the sentences.

sure	have	scissors

1 나는 가위가 필요해요.

I need ＿＿＿＿＿＿＿.

2 나는 연필과 종이를 가지고 있어요.

I ＿＿＿＿＿＿＿ a pencil and some paper.

3 나는 비가 오지 않을 거라고 확신해요.

I'm ＿＿＿＿＿＿＿ it won't rain.

Neighborhood

Check Up Read and check the words you don't know.

1차 복습

- [ ] scissors
- [ ] paper
- [ ] rock
- [ ] have
- [ ] basket
- [ ] shape
- [ ] popular
- [ ] sure

2차 복습

- [ ] teach
- [ ] study
- [ ] classroom
- [ ] task

3차 복습

- [ ] say
- [ ] show
- [ ] journal
- [ ] catch

※ 망각 제로! 1일 전 3일 전 7일 전 학습한 단어를 복습해요.

Word Tip

scissors 가위	paper 종이	rock 바위, 돌	have 가지다
basket 바구니	shape 모양	popular 인기 있는	sure 확신하는
teach 가르치다	study 공부하다	classroom 교실	task 일, 과제
say 말하다	show 보여 주다, 공연	journal 잡지, 신문	catch 잡다

Who's the culprit?

Pop Quiz Choose and check the right words.

She came out after hearing the bell, but there was no one there.

아주머니가 _____ 소리를 듣고 나가면, 아무도 없었어요.

- [ ] 초인종
- [ ] 모퉁이

Her house is at this corner.

아주머니의 _____ 은 모퉁이에 있어요.

- [ ] 집
- [ ] 시계

Catch Up

Listen, say, and color.

Write the Basic Words and Jump Up Words.

bell 초인종, 종	**He rings the bell.** ⓝ 그가 초인종을 눌러요.

gate 대문, 문	**He opens the gate.** ⓝ 그가 대문을 열어요.

house 집	**There are four rooms in his house.** ⓝ 그의 집에는 방이 4개 있어요.

clock
시계

She looked at the clock. n

그녀는 시계를 봤어요.

corner
모퉁이

She is waiting at the corner for the bus. n

그녀는 모퉁이에서 버스를 기다리고 있어요.

damage
피해, 훼손하다

There was damage to the house. n v

집에 피해가 있었어요.

destroy
파괴하다

The house was destroyed by fire. v

그 집은 화재로 파괴되었어요.

trouble
문제, 골칫거리

I'm having trouble with my car. n

내 차에 문제가 있어요.

Skill UP

A Circle the letters and complete the words.

1

d g t k

_ a _ e

대문, 문

2

k c r l

_ _ o c k

시계

3

a o e u

h _ _ s e

집

B Find, circle, and write the words.

모퉁이	couner corner cornor

피해, 훼손하다	damage demege demage

문제, 골칫거리	trabule trouble trauble

파괴하다	distroy distray destroy

C Connect, choose, and complete the sentences.

corner	bell	damage

1

집에 피해가 있었어요.

- There was _____ to the house.

2

그가 초인종을 눌러요.

He rings the _____ .

3

그녀는 모퉁이에서 버스를 기다리고 있어요.

- She is waiting at the _____ for the bus.

D Circle the words and complete the sentences.

1 그가 대문을 열어요.

gate   house

He opens the _____ .

2 내 차에 문제가 있어요.

trouble   damage

I'm having _____ with my car.

Check Up Read and check the words you don't know.

- [ ] bell
- [ ] gate
- [ ] house
- [ ] clock

- [ ] corner
- [ ] damage
- [ ] destroy
- [ ] trouble

- [ ] visit
- [ ] sleep

- [ ] pack
- [ ] sense

- [ ] airplane
- [ ] boat

- [ ] ship
- [ ] float

※ 망각 제로! 1일 전 3일 전 7일 전 학습한 단어를 복습해요.

bell 초인종, 종   gate 대문, 문   house 집   clock 시계

corner 모퉁이   damage 피해, 훼손하다   destroy 파괴하다   trouble 문제, 골칫거리

visit 방문하다   sleep 자다   pack (짐을) 싸다, 꾸러미   sense 감각

airplane 비행기   boat 보트, (작은) 배   ship (큰) 배, 선박   float 뜨다

It's time to paint.

![Pop Quiz] **Choose and check the right words.**

They are painting on canvases.

친구들이 캔버스에 그림을 _____ 있어요.

- [ ] 그리다
- [ ] 섞다

Rod needs pink paint.

로드는 _____ 물감이 필요해요.

- [ ] 분홍색(의)
- [ ] 흰색(의)

Catch UP

Listen, say, and color.

Read & Write

Write the **Basic Words** and **Jump Up Words**.

gray
회색(의)

The cat is gray.

고양이는 회색이에요.

a n

---

brown
갈색(의)

The horse is brown.

말은 갈색이에요.

a n

---

white
흰색(의)

She's wearing a white dress.

그녀는 하얀 드레스를 입고 있어요.

a n

pink
분홍색(의)

My favorite color is pink. (a) (n)

내가 좋아하는 색은 분홍색이에요.

---

paint
칠하다, 그리다

We painted the wall white. (v)

우리는 벽을 흰색으로 칠했어요.

---

mix
섞다

Mix blue and yellow to get green. (v)

초록색이 되게 파란색과 노란색을 섞으세요.

---

frame
액자, 틀

I put the picture in a frame. (n)

나는 액자에 사진을 넣었어요.

---

canvas
캔버스 (천)

He painted on a canvas. (n)

그는 캔버스에 그림을 그렸어요.

A Circle and write the words.

1

brown : gray

_____

회색(의)

2

paint : mix

_____

칠하다

3

pink : white

_____

분홍색(의)

B Unscramble and write the words.

1 갈색(의)

w o b r n

_____

2 흰색(의)

i w t e h

_____

3 액자, 틀

e f a m r

_____

4 캔버스 (천)

a c n a v s

_____

C Connect and fill in the blanks.

① The horse is brown.

말은 _____이에요.

② I put the picture in a frame.

나는 _____에 사진을 넣었어요.

③ Mix blue and yellow to get green.

초록색이 되게 파란색과 노란색을 _____.

D Choose and complete the sentences.

| canvas | pink | gray |

① 내가 좋아하는 색은 분홍색이에요.

My favorite color is _____.

② 그는 캔버스에 그림을 그렸어요.

He painted on a _____.

③ 고양이는 회색이에요.

The cat is _____.

Check Up Read and check the words you don't know.

1차 복습

☐ gray	☐ paint
☐ brown	☐ mix
☐ white	☐ frame
☐ pink	☐ canvas

2차 복습

☐ scissors	☐ popular
☐ paper	☐ sure

3차 복습

☐ know	☐ novel
☐ write	☐ name

※ 망각 제로! 1일 전 3일 전 7일 전 학습한 단어를 복습해요.

 **Word Tip**

gray 회색(의)	**brown** 갈색(의)	**white** 흰색(의)	**pink** 분홍색(의)
paint 칠하다, 그리다	**mix** 섞다	**frame** 액자, 틀	**canvas** 캔버스 (천)
scissors 가위	**paper** 종이	**popular** 인기 있는	**sure** 확신하는
know 알다	**write** 쓰다	**novel** 소설	**name** 이름

Let's cook together!

PoP Quiz Choose and check the right words.

Dad is cutting vegetables.

아빠가 채소를 _____ 있어요.

☐ 나누다

☐ 자르다

Dennis puts the fried vegetables and shrimp on the rice.

데니스는 밥 위에 튀김을 _____.

☐ 놓다

☐ 타다

 Listen, say, and color.

 Write the **Basic Words** and **Jump Up Words**.

| **burn** 타다, 화상을 입다 | **I burned the toast.** 토스트를 태웠어요.  |

| **heat** 열기, 열 | **The heat is melting the butter.** 열기가 버터를 녹이고 있어요.  |

| **fry** (기름에) 튀기다 | **Fry the onions for five minutes.** 양파를 5분 동안 튀기세요.  |

104

put
놀다

Please put the spoon on the table. (v)

숟가락을 테이블 위에 놀아주세요.

cut
자르다, 베다

He is cutting a carrot. (v)

그는 당근을 자르고 있어요.

handle
손잡이,
다루다

The knife has a wooden handle. (n v)

그 칼은 나무 손잡이가 있어요.

share
나누다,
공유하다

We shared the pizza. (v)

우리는 피자를 나눠 먹었어요.

separate
분리하다,
분리된

Separate them into two groups. (v a)

그것들을 두 그룹으로 분리하세요.

Skill UP

A Circle and trace the words.

1 자르다 : 놓다

cut

2 튀기다 : 나누다

fry

3 타다 : 분리하다

separate

B Connect and write the words.

1 share •

2 handle •

3 burn •

4 put •

• 손잡이,
다루다

• 타다,
화상을 입다

• 나누다,
공유하다

• 놓다

C Connect, choose, and complete the sentences.

handle	burned	shared

1

그 칼은 나무 손잡이가 있어요.

The knife has a wooden

_____.

2

나는 토스트를 태웠어요.

I _____ the toast.

3

우리는 피자를 나눠 먹었어요.

We _____ the pizza.

D Circle the words and complete the sentences.

1 열기가 버터를 녹이고 있어요.

handle	heat

The _____ is melting the butter.

2 그것들을 두 그룹으로 분리하세요.

Separate	Cut

_____ them into two groups.

WORD SEARCH Find, circle, and write the words.

Word Bank

sleep · canvas
bell · paper
visit · brown
fry · scissors
heat · gate

visit

 **visit** 방문하다	**sleep** 자다	**lamp** 램프, 등	**join** 함께 하다, 가입하다	**joy** 기쁨, 즐거움
warn 경고하다, 주의를 주다	**pack** (짐을) 싸다, 꾸러미	**sense** 감각	**scissors** 가위	**paper** 종이
rock 바위, 돌	**have** 가지다	**basket** 바구니	**shape** 모양	**popular** 인기 있는
 **sure** 확신하는	**bell** 초인종, 종	 **gate** 대문, 문	**house** 집	**clock** 시계
corner 모퉁이	**damage** 피해, 훼손하다	**destroy** 파괴하다	 **trouble** 문제, 골칫거리	**gray** 회색(의)
brown 갈색(의)	**white** 흰색(의)	**pink** 분홍색(의)	 **paint** 칠하다, 그리다	**mix** 섞다
 **frame** 액자, 틀	**canvas** 캔버스 (천)	**burn** 타다, 화상을 입다	 **heat** 열기, 열	**fry** (기름에) 튀기다
put 놓다	**cut** 자르다, 베다	**handle** 손잡이, 다루다	 **share** 나누다, 공유하다	**separate** 분리하다, 분리된

Day 11~15

맞힌 개수 : ☐ / 40

❶ visit		㉑ 램프, 등	
❷ join		㉒ 자다	
❸ pack		㉓ 감각	
❹ warn		㉔ 기쁨, 즐거움	
❺ scissors		㉕ 바위, 돌	
❻ paper		㉖ 가지다	
❼ basket		㉗ 인기 있는	
❽ shape		㉘ 확신하는	
❾ bell		㉙ 집	
❿ gate		㉚ 시계	
⓫ corner		㉛ 파괴하다	
⓬ damage		㉜ 문제, 골칫거리	
⓭ gray		㉝ 흰색(의)	
⓮ brown		㉞ 분홍색(의)	
⓯ paint		㉟ 액자, 틀	
⓰ mix		㊱ 캔버스 (천)	
⓱ burn		㊲ (기름에) 튀기다	
⓲ share		㊳ 놓다	
⓳ cut		㊴ 열기, 열	
⓴ handle		㊵ 분리하다, 분리된	

Part 4

FINISH

START

Day 16 Outdoor Activities

Check Up Read and check the words you don't know.

- [ ] burn
- [ ] heat
- [ ] fry
- [ ] put
- [ ] cut
- [ ] handle
- [ ] share
- [ ] separate

- [ ] bell
- [ ] gate
- [ ] destroy
- [ ] trouble

- [ ] teacher
- [ ] student
- [ ] school
- [ ] classroom

※ 망각 제로! 1일 전 3일 전 7일 전 학습한 단어를 복습해요.

Word Tip

burn 타다, 화상을 입다
cut 자르다, 베다
bell 초인종, 종
teacher 선생님

heat 열기, 열
handle 손잡이, 다루다
gate 대문, 문
student 학생

fry (기름에) 튀기다
share 나누다, 공유하다
destroy 파괴하다
school 학교

put 놓다
separate 분리하다, 분리된
trouble 문제, 골칫거리
classroom 교실

We're here for camping!

Pop Quiz Choose and check the right words.

Rod's dad uses the hammer.

로드의 아빠는 망치를 _____.

☐ 보다

☐ 사용하다

Lucia is careful not to get hurt.

루시아는 _____ 않도록 조심해요.

☐ 원하다

☐ 다치다

Read & Write Write the **Basic Words** and **Jump Up Words**.

use 사용하다	**Use my camping chair.** 제 캠핑 의자를 사용하세요. _____ - - - - - - - - - - - - - - - - - - - _____

look 보다	**Look at the sky.** 하늘을 보세요. _____ - - - - - - - - - - - - - - - - - - - _____

help 돕다	**I helped him put up the tent.** 나는 그가 텐트 치는 것을 도왔어요. _____ - - - - - - - - - - - - - - - - - - - _____

want
원하다

I want to go camping.

나는 캠핑 가길 원해요.

---

draw
그리다

Draw a flower with crayons.

크레용으로 꽃을 그리세요.

---

hurt
다친,
다치게 하다

Be careful not to get hurt.

다치지 않게 조심하세요.

---

role
역할, 배역

His role is the leader.

그의 역할은 리더예요.

---

steady
꾸준한

We have made steady progress.

우리는 꾸준한 발전을 이루었어요.

3 km   10 km   20 km

A Circle the letters and complete the words.

1

g h f p

_ e l

돕다

2

a o u k

l _ o

보다

3

w r u l

h _ t

다친, 다치게 하다

B Unscramble and write the words.

1 사용하다

s u e

2 그리다

d a w r

3 원하다

n a w t

4 꾸준한

a t e s y d

C Connect and fill in the blanks.

1

Draw **a flower with crayons.**

크레용으로 꽃을 _____.

2

His **role** is the leader.

그의 _____은 리더예요.

3

Use **my camping chair.**

제 캠핑 의자를 _____.

D Choose and complete the sentences.

hurt	want	steady

1 다치지 않게 조심하세요.

Be careful not to get _____.

2 나는 캠핑 가길 원해요.

I _____ to go camping.

3 우리는 꾸준한 발전을 이루었어요.

We have made _____ progress.

Day 17 Finance

Check Up Read and check the words you don't know.

1차 복습

- ☐ use
- ☐ look
- ☐ help
- ☐ want
- ☐ draw
- ☐ hurt
- ☐ role
- ☐ steady

2차 복습

- ☐ gray
- ☐ brown
- ☐ frame
- ☐ canvas

3차 복습

- ☐ lamp
- ☐ join
- ☐ joy
- ☐ warn

※ 망각 제로! 1일 전 3일 전 7일 전 학습한 단어를 복습해요.

Word Tip

use 사용하다	**look** 보다	**help** 돕다	**want** 원하다
draw 그리다	**hurt** 다친, 다치게 하다	**role** 역할, 배역	**steady** 꾸준한
gray 회색(의)	**brown** 갈색(의)	**frame** 액자, 틀	**canvas** 캔버스 (천)
lamp 램프, 등	**join** 함께 하다, 가입하다	**joy** 기쁨, 즐거움	**warn** 경고하다, 주의를 주다

Don't waste your money.

POP Quiz Choose and check the right words.

Kiara has no money.

키아라는 _____이 하나도 없어요.

☐ 돈

☐ 가게

Don't waste your money.

돈을 _____면 안 돼요.

☐ 낭비하다

☐ 믿다

Read & Write Write the **Basic Words** and **Jump Up Words**.

money 돈	**I have money.** <small>n</small> 나는 돈이 있어요.

buy 사다	**I buy a pencil.** <small>v</small> 나는 연필을 사요.

store 가게, 상점	**I go to the toy store.** <small>n</small> 나는 장난감 가게에 가요.

poor
가난한

He is poor.

그는 가난해요.

_____

- - - - - - - - - - -

_____

rich
부자인, 부유한

She is rich.

그녀는 부자예요.

_____

- - - - - - - - - - -

_____

fortune
거금, 운, 재산

They made a fortune.

그들은 거금을 벌었어요.

_____

- - - - - - - - - - -

_____

trust
믿다, 신뢰

I lend money to people I trust.

나는 믿는 사람들에게 돈을 빌려줘요.

_____

- - - - - - - - - - -

_____

waste
낭비하다

We wasted **a lot of money.**

우리는 많은 돈을 낭비했어요.

_____

- - - - - - - - - - -

_____

Skill UP

A Circle and trace the words.

1 부유한 | 가난한

rich

2 가게 | 돈

money

3 믿다 | 낭비하다

waste

B Find, circle, and write the words.

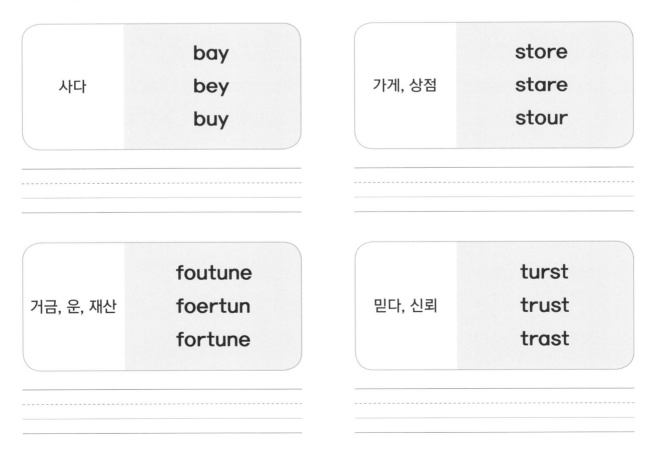

사다
bay
bey
buy

가게, 상점
store
stare
stour

거금, 운, 재산
foutune
foertun
fortune

믿다, 신뢰
turst
trust
trast

C Connect, choose, and complete the sentences.

store	poor	fortune

1

그는 가난해요.

He is _____.

2

그들은 거금을 벌었어요.

They made a _____.

3

나는 장난감 가게에 가요.

I go to the toy _____.

D Circle the words and complete the sentences.

1 나는 믿는 사람들에게 돈을 빌려줘요.

fortune	trust

I lend money to people I _____.

2 나는 연필을 사요.

waste	buy

I _____ a pencil.

Day 18 Body & Actions

Check Up Read and check the words you don't know.

1차 복습

- [ ] money
- [ ] buy
- [ ] store
- [ ] poor
- [ ] rich
- [ ] fortune
- [ ] trust
- [ ] waste

2차 복습

- [ ] burn
- [ ] heat
- [ ] share
- [ ] separate

3차 복습

- [ ] rock
- [ ] have
- [ ] basket
- [ ] shape

※ **망각 제로!** 1일 전 3일 전 7일 전 학습한 단어를 복습해요.

Word Tip

money 돈
rich 부자인, 부유한
burn 타다, 화상을 입다
rock 바위, 돌

buy 사다
fortune 거금, 운, 재산
heat 열기, 열
have 가지다

store 가게, 상점
trust 믿다, 신뢰
share 나누다, 공유하다
basket 바구니

poor 가난한
waste 낭비하다
separate 분리하다, 분리된
shape 모양

124

Isn't she lovely?

Choose and check the right words.

Lily's red cheeks are so cute.

릴리의 발그레한 _____이 정말 귀여워요.

- [ ] 뺨
- [ ] 발

Kiara looks at Lily's tiny teeth.

키아라는 릴리의 작은 _____를 봐요.

- [ ] 이, 치아
- [ ] 몸, 신체

Catch Up

Read & Write Write the **Basic Words** and **Jump Up Words**.

hand 손	**Look at my hands.** 내 손을 보세요. —————————— —————————— ——————————

foot 발	**I wash my foot.** 나는 발을 씻어요. —————————— —————————— ——————————

tooth 이, 치아	**He lost a tooth.** 그는 이가 빠졌어요. —————————— —————————— ——————————

body
몸, 신체

Blood flows through the body. n

혈액은 몸을 통해 흘러요.

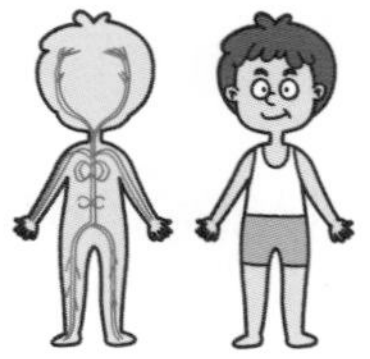

---

lips
입술

She has red lips. n

그녀는 입술이 빨개요.

---

cheek
뺨, 볼

He has rosy cheeks. n

그는 뺨이 장밋빛이에요.

---

physical
육체의, 물질의

He is in physical pain. a

그는 육체적으로 고통을 겪고 있어요.

---

pull
당기다, 뽑다

Please pull the rope. v

밧줄을 당겨 주세요.

A Circle and write the words.

1

foot	hand

_____

손

2

cheek	lips

_____

뺨, 볼

3

tooth	body

_____

이, 치아

B Unscramble and write the words.

1 몸, 신체   y o d b   _____

2 입술   s i l p   _____

3 육체의,
물질의   h p y s i l a c   _____

4 당기다,
뽑다   l p u l   _____

C Connect and fill in the blanks.

1

Blood flows through the body.

혈액은 _____을 통해 흘러요.

2

I wash my foot.

나는 _____을 씻어요.

3

She has red lips.

그녀는 _____이 빨개요.

D Choose and complete the sentences.

tooth	pull	physical

1 그는 이가 빠졌어요.

He lost a _____.

2 그는 육체적으로 고통을 겪고 있어요.

He is in _____ pain.

3 밧줄을 당겨 주세요.

Please _____ the rope.

Day 19 Sports

1차 복습

- [ ] hand
- [ ] foot
- [ ] tooth
- [ ] body
- [ ] lips
- [ ] cheek
- [ ] physical
- [ ] pull

2차 복습

- [ ] use
- [ ] look
- [ ] role
- [ ] steady

3차 복습

- [ ] house
- [ ] clock
- [ ] corner
- [ ] damage

※ 망각 제로! 1일 전 3일 전 7일 전 학습한 단어를 복습해요.

 Word Tip

hand 손	**foot** 발	**tooth** 이, 치아	**body** 몸, 신체
lips 입술	**cheek** 뺨, 볼	**physical** 육체의, 물질의	**pull** 당기다, 뽑다
use 사용하다	**look** 보다	**role** 역할, 배역	**steady** 꾸준한
house 집	**clock** 시계	**corner** 모퉁이	**damage** 피해, 훼손하다

What a game!

데니스와 로드가 축구 경기를 하고 있어요.
Dennis and Rod are playing in a football game.

Pop Quiz Choose and check the right words.

Dennis and Rod are playing football.

데니스와 로드가 _____ 경기를 하고 있어요.

☐ 축구

☐ 농구

Rod's friends are so proud of him.

로드의 친구들은 그가 매우 _____요.

☐ 인기 있는

☐ 자랑스러운

Read & Write

 Write the **Basic Words** and **Jump Up Words**.

---

kick

(발로) 차다

I kick the ball.

나는 공을 (발로) 차요.

_____

---

touch

만지다

Don't touch it.

그것을 만지지 마세요.

_____

---

roll

구르다

We roll a ball in bowling.

우리는 볼링에서 공을 굴려요.

_____

132

hit
치다, 때리다

I hit the ball. ⓥ

나는 공을 쳐요.

_____

- - - - - - - - - - - - -

_____

football
축구

We enjoy playing football. ⓝ

우리는 축구하는 것을 즐겨요.

_____

- - - - - - - - - - - - -

_____

cheer
환호성,
응원하다

A deafening cheer went up. ⓝ ⓥ

귀청이 찢어질 듯한 환호성이 터졌어요.

_____

- - - - - - - - - - - - -

_____

hug
껴안다,
포옹하다

They hugged each other after the game. ⓥ

그들은 경기 후에 서로 껴안았어요.

_____

- - - - - - - - - - - - -

_____

proud
자랑스러운

I'm proud of you. ⓐ

나는 네가 자랑스러워.

_____

- - - - - - - - - - - - -

_____

A Circle the letters and complete the words.

1

c　k　p　g

_ i _ k

(발로) 차다

2

a　o　u　e

h _ g

껴안다, 포옹하다

3 Marathon

q　r　p　w

_ _ o u d

자랑스러운

B Connect and write the words.

1 football　•

2 roll　•

3 cheer　•

4 touch　•

•　만지다

•　환호성, 응원하다

•　축구

•　구르다

_____

_____

_____

_____

C Connect and fill in the blanks.

1

A deafening cheer went up.

귀청이 찢어질 듯한 _____이 터졌어요.

2

We roll a ball in bowling.

우리는 볼링에서 공을 _____.

3

We enjoy playing football.

우리는 _____하는 것을 즐겨요.

D Circle the words and complete the sentences.

1 나는 공을 쳐요.

hug	hit

I _____ the ball.

2 그것을 만지지 마세요.

touch	kick

Don't _____ it.

Day 20 Travel

Check Up Read and check the words you don't know.

1차 복습

- [ ] kick
- [ ] touch
- [ ] roll
- [ ] hit
- [ ] football
- [ ] cheer
- [ ] hug
- [ ] proud

2차 복습

- [ ] money
- [ ] buy
- [ ] trust
- [ ] waste

3차 복습

- [ ] white
- [ ] pink
- [ ] paint
- [ ] mix

※ **망각 제로!** 1일 전 3일 전 7일 전 학습한 단어를 복습해요.

Word Tip

kick (발로) 차다	**touch** 만지다	**roll** 구르다	**hit** 치다, 때리다
football 축구	**cheer** 환호성, 응원하다	**hug** 껴안다, 포옹하다	**proud** 자랑스러운
money 돈	**buy** 사다	**trust** 믿다, 신뢰	**waste** 낭비하다
white 흰색(의)	**pink** 분홍색(의)	**paint** 칠하다, 그리다	**mix** 섞다

Sally likes to travel.

Pop Quiz — Choose and check the right words.

Sally shows Kiara her travel diary.

샐리가 키아라에게 여행 ＿＿＿＿＿＿＿를 보여줘요.

- [ ] 일기
- [ ] 지도

Sally wants to sail around the world someday.

샐리는 언젠가 전 세계를 ＿＿＿＿＿＿＿ 싶어요.

- [ ] 비행하다
- [ ] 항해하다

137

 **Listen, say, and color.**

 Write the Basic Words and Jump Up Words.

| drive
운전하다 | **He drives on trips.** ⓥ |
| | 그는 여행 중에 운전해요. |

| fly
날다,
비행하다 | **We always fly to Canada.** ⓥ |
| | 우리는 항상 캐나다로 날아가요. |

| map
지도 | **She looks at a map.** ⓝ |
| | 그녀는 지도를 봐요. |

travel
여행하다, 여행

We travel **by bus.** ⓥ ⓝ

우리는 버스로 여행해요.

---

diary
일기

I kept a travel diary**.** ⓝ

나는 여행 일기를 썼어요.

---

sail
항해하다, 돛

I sail **around the world.** ⓥ ⓝ

나는 전 세계를 항해해요.

---

leave
떠나다,
출발하다

The bus is leaving **the station.** ⓥ

버스가 역을 떠나고 있어요.

---

wave
(손을) 흔들다,
물결

They waved **at me.** ⓥ ⓝ

그들은 나에게 손을 흔들었어요.

Skill Up

A Circle and write the words.

1 wave : leave

떠나다, 출발하다

2 map : diary

지도

3 drive : sail

운전하다

B Find, circle, and write the words.

(손을) 흔들다, 물결	weve wave weva

일기	dairy diary daily

여행하다, 여행	trevel traval travel

항해하다, 돛	sail seil sale

C Connect, choose, and complete the sentences.

diary	travel	fly

1

우리는 버스로 여행해요.

We _____ by bus.

2

나는 여행 일기를 썼어요.

I kept a travel _____.

3

우리는 항상 캐나다로 날아가요.

We always _____ to Canada.

D Choose and complete the sentences.

sail	waved	map

1 그녀는 지도를 봐요.

She looks at a _____.

2 나는 전 세계를 항해해요.

I _____ around the world.

3 그들은 나에게 손을 흔들었어요.

They _____ at me.

WORD PUZZLE

Complete the word puzzle.
Then write the sentence.

Word Bank

look · help · trust · store · lips
pull · cheer · roll · map · wave

t _ r _ u _ s _ t

use 사용하다	**look** 보다	**help** 돕다	**want** 원하다	**draw** 그리다
hurt 다친, 다치게 하다	**role** 역할, 배역	**steady** 꾸준한	**money** 돈	**buy** 사다
store 가게, 상점	**poor** 가난한	**rich** 부자인, 부유한	**fortune** 거금, 운, 재산	**trust** 믿다, 신뢰
waste 낭비하다	**hand** 손	**foot** 발	**tooth** 이, 치아	**body** 몸, 신체
lips 입술	**cheek** 뺨, 볼	**physical** 육체의, 물질의	**pull** 당기다, 뽑다	**kick** (발로) 차다
touch 만지다	**roll** 구르다	**hit** 치다, 때리다	**football** 축구	**cheer** 환호성, 응원하다
hug 껴안다, 포옹하다	**proud** 자랑스러운	**drive** 운전하다	**fly** 날다, 비행하다	**map** 지도
travel 여행하다, 여행	**diary** 일기	**sail** 항해하다, 돛	**leave** 떠나다, 출발하다	**wave** (손을) 흔들다, 물결

Day 16~20

맞힌 개수 : ___ / 40

❶ use		㉑ 돕다	
❷ look		㉒ 원하다	
❸ draw		㉓ 역할, 배역	
❹ hurt		㉔ 꾸준한	
❺ money		㉕ 가게, 상점	
❻ buy		㉖ 가난한	
❼ rich		㉗ 믿다, 신뢰	
❽ fortune		㉘ 낭비하다	
❾ hand		㉙ 이, 치아	
❿ foot		㉚ 몸, 신체	
⓫ lips		㉛ 육체의, 물질의	
⓬ cheek		㉜ 당기다, 뽑다	
⓭ kick		㉝ 구르다	
⓮ touch		㉞ 치다, 때리다	
⓯ hug		㉟ 축구	
⓰ cheer		㊱ 자랑스러운	
⓱ wave		㊲ 지도	
⓲ fly		㊳ 여행하다, 여행	
⓳ leave		㊴ 일기	
⓴ sail		㊵ 운전하다	

Part 5

FINISH

START

Check Up Read and check the words you don't know.

1차 복습

- [ ] drive
- [ ] fly
- [ ] map
- [ ] travel
- [ ] diary
- [ ] sail
- [ ] leave
- [ ] wave

2차 복습

- [ ] hand
- [ ] foot
- [ ] physical
- [ ] pull

3차 복습

- [ ] fry
- [ ] put
- [ ] cut
- [ ] handle

※ 망각 제로! 1일 전 3일 전 7일 전 학습한 단어를 복습해요.

Word Tip

drive 운전하다   fly 날다, 비행하다   map 지도   travel 여행하다, 여행

diary 일기   sail 항해하다, 돛   leave 떠나다, 출발하다   wave (손을) 흔들다, 물결

hand 손   foot 발   physical 육체의, 물질의   pull 당기다, 뽑다

fry (기름에) 튀기다   put 놓다   cut 자르다, 베다   handle 손잡이, 다루다

There are frogs in the pond.

POP Quiz Choose and check the right words.

A frog **is** diving **into the** pond**.**

_____가 연못으로 뛰어들고 있어요.

☐ 개미

☐ 개구리

The frog might have poison**.**

그 개구리는 _____이 있을지도 몰라요.

☐ 독

☐ 구름

Read & Write
Write the Basic Words and Jump Up Words.

---

ant
개미

The ant is carrying food.
개미가 음식을 나르고 있어요.

---

bee
벌

The bee is on a flower.
벌이 꽃 위에 있어요.

---

frog
개구리

The frog has many spots.
그 개구리는 많은 점을 가지고 있어요.

pond
연못

Frogs live in a pond. (n)

개구리는 연못에 살아요.

cloud
구름

A cloud covered the sun. (n)

구름이 해를 가렸어요.

poison
독

It contains a deadly poison. (n)

그것은 치명적인 독이 있어요.

harm
해치다, 해

Garbage may harm the environment. (v)(n)

쓰레기는 환경을 해칠 수도 있어요.

dive
(물속으로) 뛰어들다

The frog is diving into the pond. (v)

개구리가 연못으로 뛰어들고 있어요.

A Circle and trace the words.

1

개구리	개미

frog

2

구름	연못

pond

3

뛰어들다	해치다

dive

B Unscramble and write the words.

1 개미   a t n

2 해치다, 해   a h r m

3 구름   l u c o d

4 독   i s n p o o

C Connect and fill in the blanks.

1

A cloud covered the sun.

_____이 해를 가렸어요.

2

The bee is on a flower.

_____이 꽃 위에 있어요.

3

The ant is carrying food.

_____가 음식을 나르고 있어요.

D Circle the words and complete the sentences.

1 개구리는 연못에 살아요.

cloud	pond

Frogs live in a _____.

2 그것은 치명적인 독이 있어요.

poison	harm

It contains a deadly _____.

Day 22 Weather & Emotions

1차 복습

- ☐ ant
- ☐ bee
- ☐ frog
- ☐ pond
- ☐ cloud
- ☐ poison
- ☐ harm
- ☐ dive

2차 복습

- ☐ kick
- ☐ touch
- ☐ hug
- ☐ proud

3차 복습

- ☐ help
- ☐ want
- ☐ draw
- ☐ hurt

※ 망각 제로! 1일 전 3일 전 7일 전 학습한 단어를 복습해요.

ant 개미   **bee** 벌   **frog** 개구리   **pond** 연못

cloud 구름   **poison** 독   **harm** 해치다, 해   **dive** (물속으로) 뛰어들다

kick (발로) 차다   **touch** 만지다   **hug** 껴안다, 포옹하다   **proud** 자랑스러운

help 돕다   **want** 원하다   **draw** 그리다   **hurt** 다친, 다치게 하다

Rod looks so sad.

Pop Quiz Choose and check the right words.

It's been raining all day.

하루 종일 _____.

☐ 눈이 오다

☐ 비가 오다

Kiara doesn't like damp weather.

키아라는 _____ 날씨를 싫어해요.

☐ 축축한

☐ 빛나는

Listen & Say Listen, say, and color.

Read & Write Write the **Basic Words** and **Jump Up Words**.

---

snow
눈, 눈이 오다

We play in the snow. n v

우리는 눈 속에서 놀아요.

---

rain
비, 비가 오다

We play in the rain. n v

우리는 빗속에서 놀아요.

---

rainbow
무지개

Look at the rainbow in the sky. n

하늘에 떠 있는 무지개를 보세요.

154

smile
미소 짓다,
미소

He smiled at me.
그가 나에게 미소 지었어요.

v **n**

---

luck
행운

Best of luck to you!
행운을 빌어요!

n

---

damp
축축한

The shirt is still damp.
그 셔츠는 아직 축축해요.

a

---

shine
빛나다,
반짝이다

Stars shine in the sky.
별들이 하늘에서 빛나요.

v

---

view
경관, 견해

What a wonderful view!
경관이 정말 멋지군요!

n

A Circle the letters and complete the words.

1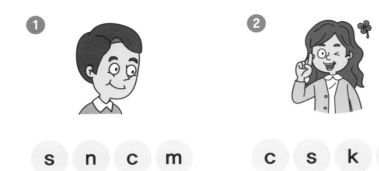

s n c m

___ i l e
미소 짓다, 미소

2

c s k t

l u ___ ___
행운

3

a e i o

r ___ ___ n
비, 비가 오다

B Connect and write the words.

1 rainbow •   • 무지개   ------------------

2 damp •   • 경관, 견해   ------------------

3 shine •   • 빛나다, 반짝이다   ------------------

4 view •   • 축축한   ------------------

C Connect and fill in the blanks.

1

Stars shine **in the sky.**

별들이 하늘에서 _____.

2

The shirt is still damp.

그 셔츠는 아직 _____.

3

We play in the snow.

우리는 _____ 속에서 놀아요.

D Choose and complete the sentences.

view	rainbow	luck

1 하늘에 떠 있는 무지개를 보세요.

Look at the _____ **in the sky.**

2 행운을 빌어요!

Best of _____ **to you!**

3 경관이 정말 멋지군요!

What a wonderful _____!

Check Up Read and check the words you don't know.

1차 복습

- [ ] snow
- [ ] rain
- [ ] rainbow
- [ ] smile

- [ ] luck
- [ ] damp
- [ ] shine
- [ ] view

2차 복습

- [ ] drive
- [ ] fly

- [ ] leave
- [ ] wave

3차 복습

- [ ] store
- [ ] poor

- [ ] rich
- [ ] fortune

※ **망각 제로!** 1일 전 3일 전 7일 전 학습한 단어를 복습해요.

snow 눈, 눈이 오다	**rain** 비, 비가 오다	**rainbow** 무지개	**smile** 미소 짓다, 미소
luck 행운	**damp** 축축한	**shine** 빛나다, 반짝이다	**view** 경관, 견해
drive 운전하다	**fly** 날다, 비행하다	**leave** 떠나다, 출발하다	**wave** (손을) 흔들다, 물결
store 가게, 상점	**poor** 가난한	**rich** 부자인, 부유한	**fortune** 거금, 운, 재산

What should we bring to the desert?

Pop Quiz Choose and check the right words.

The desert is cold at night.

_____은 밤에 추워요.

- [ ] 해안
- [ ] 사막

Rod and Mong need warm clothes.

로드와 몽은 _____ 옷이 필요해요.

- [ ] 추운
- [ ] 따뜻한

Read & Write Write the **Basic Words** and **Jump Up Words**.

hot 더운	**It's hot in summer.** 여름에는 더워요.

cold 추운	**It's cold in winter.** 겨울에는 추워요.

warm 따뜻한	**It's warm in spring.** 봄에는 따뜻해요.

ice
얼음

He slipped on the ice. n

그는 얼음 위에서 미끄러졌어요.

water
물

There is a lot of water in our country. n

우리나라에는 많은 물이 있어요.

shore
해안, 호숫가

I'm swimming to the shore. n

나는 해안으로 헤엄쳐 가고 있어요.

desert
사막

The desert is hot and dry. n

사막은 덥고 건조해요.

island
섬

We live on a small island. n

우리는 작은 섬에 살아요.

A Circle and write the words.

1

hot	cold

_____

추운

2

water	ice

_____

물

3

desert	shore

_____

사막

B Unscramble and write the words.

1 해안,
호숫가   h s r o e   _____

2 섬   s i l n a d   _____

3 따뜻한   a w r m   _____

4 얼음   e i c   _____

C Connect, choose, and complete the sentences.

shore	island	hot

1

나는 해안으로 헤엄쳐 가고 있어요.

I'm swimming to the _____.

2

우리는 작은 섬에 살아요.

We live on a small _____.

3

여름에는 더워요.

It's _____ in summer.

D Circle the words and complete the sentences.

1 봄에는 따뜻해요.

warm cold

It's _____ in spring.

2 사막은 덥고 건조해요.

island desert

The _____ is hot and dry.

Day 24 Clothes

Check Up Read and check the words you don't know.

1차 복습

☐ hot	☐ water
☐ cold	☐ shore
☐ warm	☐ desert
☐ ice	☐ island

2차 복습

☐ ant	☐ harm
☐ bee	☐ dive

3차 복습

☐ tooth	☐ lips
☐ body	☐ cheek

※ 망각 제로! 1일 전 3일 전 7일 전 학습한 단어를 복습해요.

hot 더운	**cold** 추운	**warm** 따뜻한	**ice** 얼음
water 물	**shore** 해안, 호숫가	**desert** 사막	**island** 섬
ant 개미	**bee** 벌	**harm** 해치다, 해	**dive** (물속으로) 뛰어들다
tooth 이, 치아	**body** 몸, 신체	**lips** 입술	**cheek** 뺨, 볼

164

What is your style?

Pop Quiz Choose and check the right words.

Kiara likes to wear trendy clothes.

키아라는 유행하는 옷을 _____ 것을 좋아해요.

- [ ] 입다
- [ ] 읽다

Rod likes a simple style.

로드는 _____ 스타일을 좋아해요.

- [ ] 단순한, 간단한
- [ ] 따뜻한

165

Catch Up

Read & Write Write the **Basic Words** and **Jump Up Words**.

pants 바지	**My pants are too long for me.** 바지가 나한테는 너무 길어요. 
socks 양말	**He's putting on socks.** 그는 양말을 신고 있어요.
wear 입다	**I wear a lot of black.** 나는 검은색 옷을 많이 입어요. 

skirt
치마

I like this blue skirt.

나는 이 파란색 치마를 좋아해요.

hat
모자

He's wearing a nice hat.

그는 멋진 모자를 쓰고 있어요.

simple
단순한, 간단한

I like simple clothes.

나는 단순한 옷을 좋아해요.

uniform
교복, 제복

We wear uniforms to school.

우리는 교복을 입고 학교에 가요.

shelf
선반, 책꽂이

Put them on the top shelf.

그것들을 맨 위 선반에 놓으세요.

A Circle and write the words.

1
pants	socks

_____

바지

2
skirt	hat

_____

모자

3
shelf	uniform

_____

교복, 제복

B Find, circle, and write the words.

입다	wear
	were
	waer

_____

선반, 책꽂이	shlef
	schef
	shelf

_____

양말	sosks
	sucks
	socks

_____

단순한, 간단한	sample
	simple
	simpel

_____

C Connect and fill in the blanks.

1.

I wear a lot of black.

나는 검은색 옷을 많이 _____ .

2.

Put them on the top shelf.

그것들을 맨 위 _____ 에 놓으세요.

3.

I like this blue skirt.

나는 이 파란색 _____ 를 좋아해요.

D Choose and complete the sentences.

| pants | socks | simple |

1. 그는 양말을 신고 있어요.

   He's putting on _____ .

2. 나는 단순한 옷을 좋아해요.

   I like _____ clothes.

3. 바지가 나한테는 너무 길어요.

   My _____ are too long for me.

Supernatural

Check Up Read and check the words you don't know.

1차 복습

☐ pants	☐ hat
☐ socks	☐ simple
☐ wear	☐ uniform
☐ skirt	☐ shelf

2차 복습

☐ snow	☐ shine
☐ rain	☐ view

3차 복습

☐ roll	☐ football
☐ hit	☐ cheer

※ **망각 제로!** 1일 전 3일 전 7일 전 학습한 단어를 복습해요.

pants 바지	**socks** 양말	**wear** 입다	**skirt** 치마
hat 모자	**simple** 단순한, 간단한	**uniform** 교복, 제복	**shelf** 선반, 책꽂이
snow 눈, 눈이 오다	**rain** 비, 비가 오다	**shine** 빛나다, 반짝이다	**view** 경관, 견해
roll 구르다	**hit** 치다, 때리다	**football** 축구	**cheer** 환호성, 응원하다

Do you believe in ghosts?

PoP QuiZ Choose and check the right words.

They just watched a horror movie.

친구들은 방금 _____ 영화를 봤어요.

☐ 천사

☐ 공포

Do we become ghosts after we die?

우리도 죽으면 _____ 이 되는 걸까?

☐ 유령

☐ 벌레

Listen & Say Listen, say, and color.

Read & Write Write the **Basic Words** and **Jump Up Words**.

die 죽다	**The man died in 1960.** 그 남자는 1960년에 죽었어요.	v 
angel 천사	**He looks like an angel.** 그는 천사처럼 보여요.	n 
cow 소	**I can talk with cows.** 나는 소와 대화할 수 있어요.	n 

pig
돼지

A pig is a symbol of good luck. (n)
돼지는 행운의 상징이에요.

bug
벌레

He can transform into a bug. (n)
그는 벌레로 변신할 수 있어요.

horror
공포

I like horror movies. (n)
나는 공포 영화를 좋아해요.

ghost
유령

I saw a ghost on the lake. (n)
나는 호수에서 유령을 봤어요.

doubt
의심하다, 의심

I doubt there are aliens. (v) (n)
나는 외계인이 있는지 의심스러워요.

Skill UP

A Circle the letters and complete the words.

1

a e i o

c _ w

소

2

e a z g

_ n _ e l

천사

3

s h g j

_ _ o s t

유령

B Connect and write the words.

1 bug •   • 죽다   _____

2 die •   • 의심하다,   _____
                        의심

3 doubt •   • 벌레   _____

4 horror •   • 공포   _____

C Connect, choose, and complete the sentences.

| horror | pig | doubt |

1 돼지는 행운의 상징이에요.

A _____ is a symbol of good luck.

2 나는 외계인이 있는지 의심스러워요.

I _____ there are aliens.

3 나는 공포 영화를 좋아해요.

I like _____ movies.

D Circle the words and complete the sentences.

1 그는 벌레로 변신할 수 있어요.

bug   ghost

He can transform into a _____ .

2 그는 천사처럼 보여요.

pig   angel

He looks like an _____ .

WORD PUZZLE Complete the word puzzle.

ACROSS

② It's _____ in spring.

⑤ A _____ covered the sun.

⑦ We play in the _____.

⑧ There is a lot of _____ in our country.

DOWN

① He's putting on _____.

③ We play in the _____.

④ I can talk with _____s.

⑥ I _____ there are aliens.

⑦ I like this blue _____.

⑨ The _____ is carrying food.

ant 개미	**bee** 벌	**frog** 개구리	**pond** 연못	**cloud** 구름
poison 독	**harm** 해치다, 해	**dive** (물속으로) 뛰어들다	**snow** 눈, 눈이 오다	**rain** 비, 비가 오다
rainbow 무지개	**smile** 미소 짓다, 미소	**luck** 행운	**damp** 축축한	**shine** 빛나다, 반짝이다
view 경관, 견해	**hot** 더운	**cold** 추운	**warm** 따뜻한	**ice** 얼음
water 물	**shore** 해안, 호숫가	**desert** 사막	**island** 섬	**pants** 바지
socks 양말	**wear** 입다	**skirt** 치마	**hat** 모자	**simple** 단순한, 간단한
uniform 교복, 제복	**shelf** 선반, 책꽂이	**die** 죽다	**angel** 천사	**cow** 소
pig 돼지	**bug** 벌레	**horror** 공포	**ghost** 유령	**doubt** 의심하다, 의심

Review TEST

맞힌 개수 : / 40

❶ ant		㉑ 개구리	
❷ bee		㉒ 연못	
❸ cloud		㉓ 해치다, 해	
❹ dive		㉔ 독	
❺ snow		㉕ 무지개	
❻ rain		㉖ 미소 짓다, 미소	
❼ luck		㉗ 빛나다, 반짝이다	
❽ damp		㉘ 경관, 견해	
❾ hot		㉙ 따뜻한	
❿ cold		㉚ 얼음	
⓫ water		㉛ 사막	
⓬ shore		㉜ 섬	
⓭ pants		㉝ 입다	
⓮ socks		㉞ 치마	
⓯ hat		㉟ 교복, 제복	
⓰ simple		㊱ 선반, 책꽂이	
⓱ die		㊲ 소	
⓲ angel		㊳ 돼지	
⓳ bug		㊴ 유령	
⓴ horror		㊵ 의심하다, 의심	

Answer Key
Level 1.2

P11

 감자 당근 배 포도

P14~15

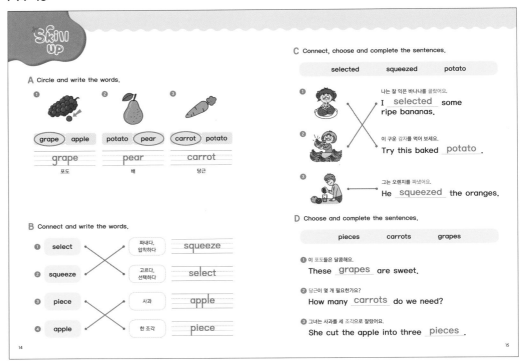

Skill Up

A Circle and write the words.

① grape apple — grape 포도
② potato pear — pear 배
③ carrot potato — carrot 당근

B Connect and write the words.

① select — 파내다, 압착하다 — squeeze
② squeeze — 고르다, 선택하다 — select
③ piece — 사과 — apple
④ apple — 한 조각 — piece

C Connect, choose and complete the sentences.

selected   squeezed   potato

① 나는 잘 익은 바나나를 골랐어요.
I __selected__ some ripe bananas.

② 이 구운 감자를 먹어 보세요.
Try this baked __potato__ .

③ 그는 오렌지를 짜냈어요.
He __squeezed__ the oranges.

D Choose and complete the sentences.

pieces   carrots   grapes

❶ 이 포도는 달콤해요.
These __grapes__ are sweet.

❷ 당근이 몇 개 필요한가요?
How many __carrots__ do we need?

❸ 그녀는 사과를 세 조각으로 잘랐어요.
She cut the apple into three __pieces__ .

14   15

P17

 선물 공포 장난감 풍선

P20~21

Skill Up

A Circle the letters and complete the words.

① a (u) i (e) — r u l e 규칙
② (f) b z (r) — f e a r 공포, 두려움
③ f k (r u) — b u r s t 터뜨리다, 터지다

B Unscramble and write the words.

❶ 공   a l b l   — ball
❷ 선물   i f t g   — gift
❸ 장난감   y o t   — toy
❹ 풍선   l a l b o o n   — balloon

C Connect, choose, and complete the sentences.

balloons   toys   balls

① 우리는 풍선을 불었어요.
We blew up the __balloons__ .

② 많은 종류의 공들이 있어요.
There are many kinds of __balls__ .

③ 그녀는 장난감을 가지고 놀고 있어요.
She is playing with her __toys__ .

D Circle the words and complete the sentences.

❶ 내 선물은 로봇이에요.   (gift) toy
__My gift is a robot.__

❷ 나는 방망이로 공을 쳤어요.   ball (bat)
__I hit the ball with a bat .__

20   21

Day 03

P23

Pop Quiz ☐ 붓다 ✔ 먹다 ✔ 맛이 ~하다 ☐ 끓이다

P26~27

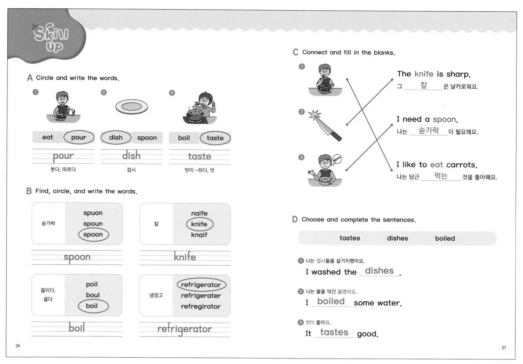

Skill Up

A Circle and write the words.

① eat (pour) pour 붓다, 따르다
② (dish) spoon dish 접시
③ boil (taste) taste 맛이 ~하다, 맛

B Find, circle, and write the words.

숟가락: spuon / spoun / (spoon) → spoon
칼: naife / (knife) / knaif → knife
끓이다, 끓다: poil / boul / (boil) → boil
냉장고: (refrigerator) / refrigerater / refregirator → refrigerator

C Connect and fill in the blanks.

① The knife is sharp.
그 __칼__ 은 날카로워요.

② I need a spoon.
나는 __숟가락__ 이 필요해요.

③ I like to eat carrots.
나는 당근 __먹는__ 것을 좋아해요.

D Choose and complete the sentences.

tastes   dishes   boiled

① 나는 접시들을 설거지했어요.
I washed the __dishes__ .

② 나는 물을 약간 끓였어요.
I __boiled__ some water.

③ 맛이 좋아요.
It __tastes__ good.

26   27

Day 04

P29

Pop Quiz ☐ 보다 ✔ 마시다 ☐ 우산 ✔ 영화

P32~33

Skill Up

A Circle and trace the words.

① 기분 (선풍기) fan
② 영화 (우산) umbrella
③ 건너뛰다 (마시다) drink

B Unscramble and write the words.

① 기분 d o m o mood
② 영화 m v i e o movie
③ 생략하다, 건너뛰다 k i p s skip
④ 전체의 h o w l e whole

C Connect and fill in the blanks.

① Let's watch a movie in my room.
내 방에서 __영화__ 를 보자.

② He's in a good mood today.
그는 오늘 __기분__ 이 좋아요.

③ He ate the whole cake.
그는 케이크를 __통째로__ 먹었어요.

D Circle the words and complete the sentences.

① 선풍기가 탁자 위에 있어요. umbrella (fan)
The __fan__ is on the table.

② 나는 오늘 밤 디저트는 생략할게요. (skip) watch
I will __skip__ dessert tonight.

32   33

P35

POP Quiz [ ] 농장 [✓] 마을 [✓] 공원 [ ] 은행

P38~39

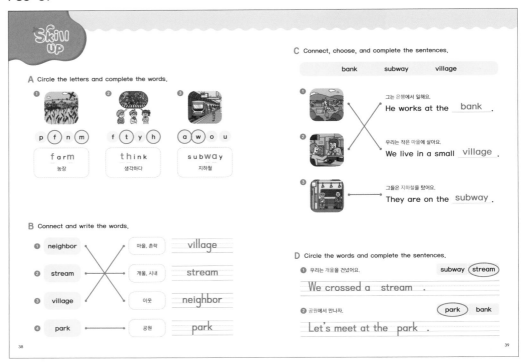

P40   P42

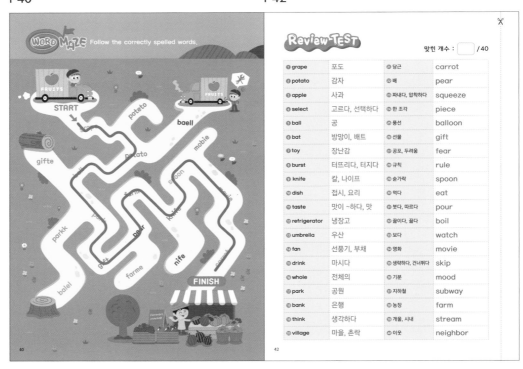

Day 06

 Pop Quiz ✓ 친절한 ☐ 현명한 ✓ 용감한 ☐ 온화한

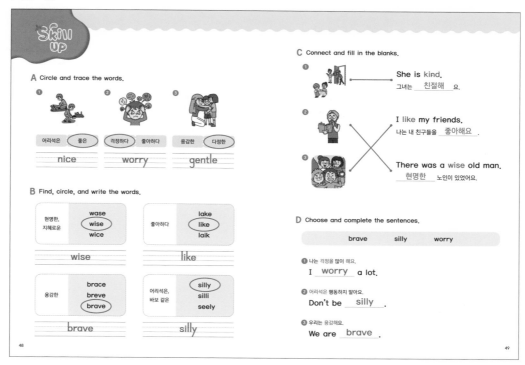

Skill UP

A Circle and trace the words.

① 어리석은 (좋은) | nice
② 걱정하다 좋아하다 | worry
③ 용감한 (다정한) | gentle

B Find, circle, and write the words.

| 현명한, 지혜로운 | wase / (wise) / wice → wise | 좋아하다 | lake / (like) / laik → like |
| 용감한 | brace / breve / (brave) → brave | 어리석은, 바보 같은 | (silly) / silli / seely → silly |

C Connect and fill in the blanks.

① She is kind.
그녀는 __친절해__ 요.

② I like my friends.
나는 내 친구들을 __좋아해요__.

③ There was a wise old man.
__현명한__ 노인이 있었어요.

D Choose and complete the sentences.

brave   silly   worry

① 나는 걱정을 많이 해요.
I __worry__ a lot.

② 어리석은 행동하지 말아요.
Don't be __silly__.

③ 우리는 용감해요.
We are __brave__.

48   49

Day 07

 Pop Quiz ☐ 말하다 ✓ 만들다 ☐ 잡다 ✓ 떨어지다

Skill UP

A Circle the letters and complete the words.

① a (e) i o → m a k e 만들다
② f (c) s h → c a t c h 잡다
③ e a i e → s e e k 찾다, 구하다

B Connect and write the words.

① leap — 여행 → journey
② journey — 떨어지다 → fall
③ fall — 말하다 → say
④ say — 뛰다, 뛰어오르다 → leap

C Connect, choose, and complete the sentences.

leap   show   journey

① 우리는 여행을 가요.
We are going on a __journey__.

② 원숭이가 나무에서 나무로 뛰어다녀요.
Monkeys __leap__ from tree to tree.

③ 나는 엄마에게 내 상을 보여 줘요.
I __show__ Mom my prize.

D Circle the words and complete the sentences.

① 의자에서 떨어지지 않도록 해.   (fall)   seek
Don't __fall__ off the chair.

② 공을 잡으세요.   Leap   (Catch)
Catch the ball, please.

54   55

Day 08

P57

Pop Quiz ☐ 배 ✓ 기차 ☐ 자동차 ✓ 비행기

P60~61

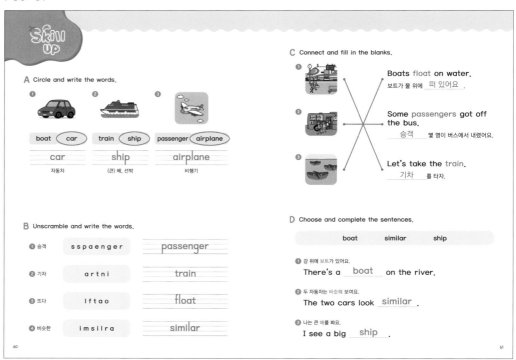

Skill Up

A Circle and write the words.

❶ boat (car)
car
자동차

❷ train (ship)
ship
(큰) 배, 선박

❸ passenger (airplane)
airplane
비행기

B Unscramble and write the words.

❶ 승객　s s p a e n g e r　passenger

❷ 기차　a r t n i　train

❸ 뜨다　l f t a o　float

❹ 비슷한　i m s i l r a　similar

C Connect and fill in the blanks.

❶ Boats float on water.
보트가 물 위에 떠 있어요.

❷ Some passengers got off the bus.
승객 몇 명이 버스에서 내렸어요.

❸ Let's take the train.
기차 를 타자.

D Choose and complete the sentences.

boat　similar　ship

❶ 강 위에 보트가 있어요.
There's a boat on the river.

❷ 두 자동차는 비슷해 보여요.
The two cars look similar.

❸ 나는 큰 배를 봐요.
I see a big ship.

60

61

Day 09

P63

Pop Quiz ☐ 소설 ✓ 잡지 ✓ 알다 ☐ 쓰다

P66~67

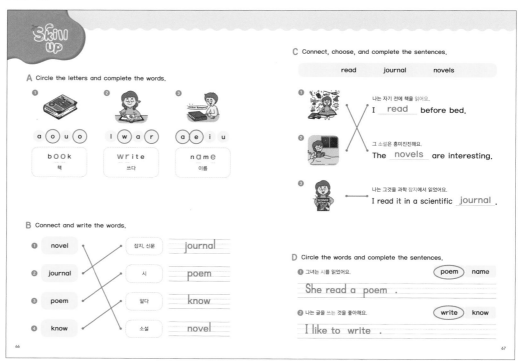

Skill Up

A Circle the letters and complete the words.

❶ a (o) u o
b o o k
책

❷ l (w a r)
w r i t e
쓰다

❸ a (e) i u
n a m e
이름

B Connect and write the words.

❶ novel → 잡지, 신문　journal

❷ journal → 시　poem

❸ poem → 알다　know

❹ know → 소설　novel

C Connect, choose, and complete the sentences.

read　journal　novels

❶ 나는 자기 전에 책을 읽어요.
I read before bed.

❷ 그 소설은 흥미진진해요.
The novels are interesting.

❸ 나는 그것을 과학 잡지에서 읽었어요.
I read it in a scientific journal.

D Circle the words and complete the sentences.

❶ 그녀는 시를 읽었어요.　(poem)　name
She read a poem.

❷ 나는 글을 쓰는 것을 좋아해요.　(write)　know
I like to write.

66

67

Pop Quiz ☑ 가르치다 ☐ 존경하다 ☐ 말하다 ☑ 공부하다

P72~73

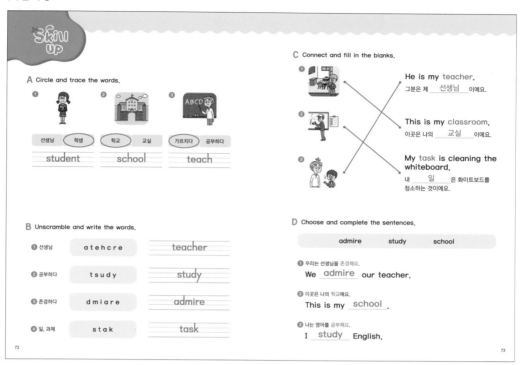

Day 06~10

P74

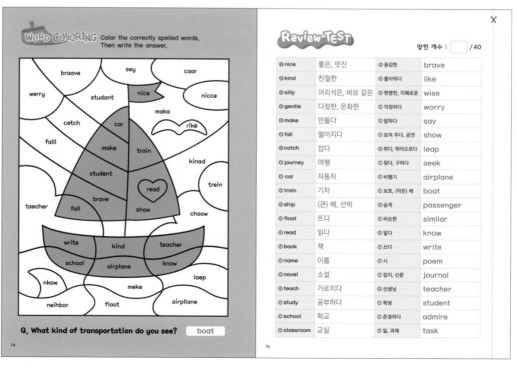

P76

Day 11

P79

 Pop Quiz ✅ 방문하다 ☐ 함께하다 ✅ 짐을 싸다 ☐ 경고하다

P82~83

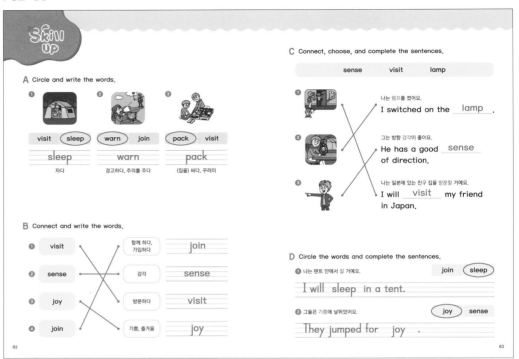

Skill Up

A Circle and write the words.

① (sleep) — sleep / 자다

② (warn) — warn / 경고하다, 주의를 주다

③ (pack) — pack / (짐을) 싸다, 꾸러미

B Connect and write the words.

① visit — 함께 하다, 가입하다 — join
② sense — 감각 — sense
③ joy — 방문하다 — visit
④ join — 기쁨, 즐거움 — joy

C Connect, choose, and complete the sentences.

| sense | visit | lamp |

① 나는 램프를 켰어요.
I switched on the **lamp**.

② 그는 방향 감각이 좋아요.
He has a good **sense** of direction.

③ 나는 일본에 있는 친구 집을 방문할 거예요.
I will **visit** my friend in Japan.

D Circle the words and complete the sentences.

① 나는 텐트 안에서 잘 거예요. join (sleep)
I will sleep in a tent.

② 그들은 기쁨에 날뛰었어요. (joy) sense
They jumped for joy.

Day 12

P85

Pop Quiz ☐ 바위 ✅ 바구니 ✅ 모양 ☐ 종이

P88~89

Skill Up

A Circle and trace the words.

① (가위) — scissors

② (모양) — shape

③ (바구니) — basket

B Unscramble and write the words.

① 종이 — e p r p a — paper
② 인기 있는 — u p l o p a r — popular
③ 바위, 돌 — o c r k — rock
④ 확신하는 — u e s r — sure

C Connect and fill in the blanks.

① They sat on a rock.
그들은 **바위** 위에 앉았어요.

② I need paper.
나는 **종이** 가 필요해요.

③ He is popular at school.
그는 학교에서 **인기 있어** 요.

D Choose and complete the sentences.

| sure | have | scissors |

① 나는 가위가 필요해요.
I need **scissors**.

② 나는 연필과 종이를 가지고 있어요.
I **have** a pencil and some paper.

③ 나는 비가 오지 않을 거라고 확신해요.
I'm **sure** it won't rain.

Day 13

P91

 ✓ 초인종 ☐ 모퉁이 ✓ 집 ☐ 시계

P94~95

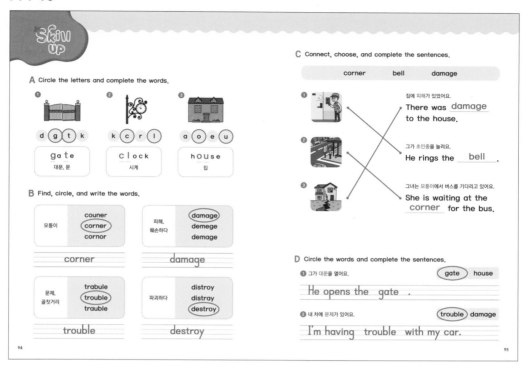

Day 14

P97

 ✓ 그리다 ☐ 섞다 ✓ 분홍색(의) ☐ 흰색(의)

P100~101

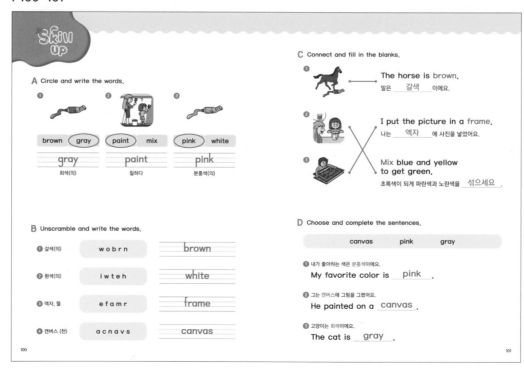

Day 15

P103

  나누다 ✓ 자르다 ✓ 놓다 타다

P106~107

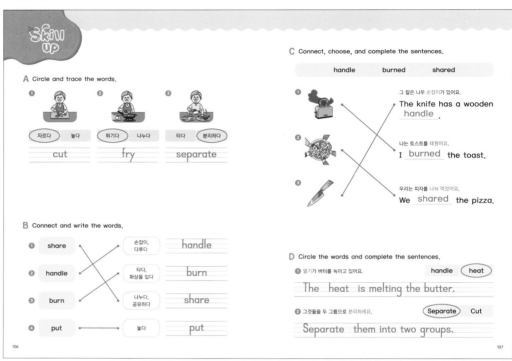

Day 11~15

P108

P110

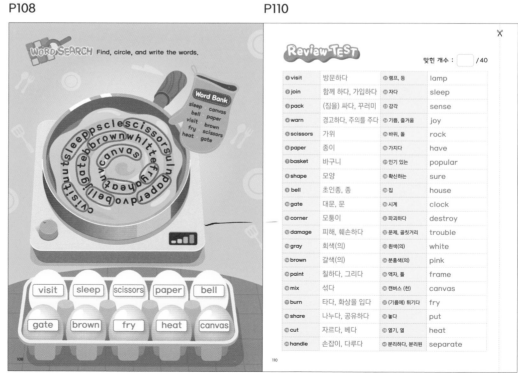

P113

 Pop Quiz [ ] 보다 [✓] 사용하다   [ ] 원하다 [✓] 다치다

P116~117

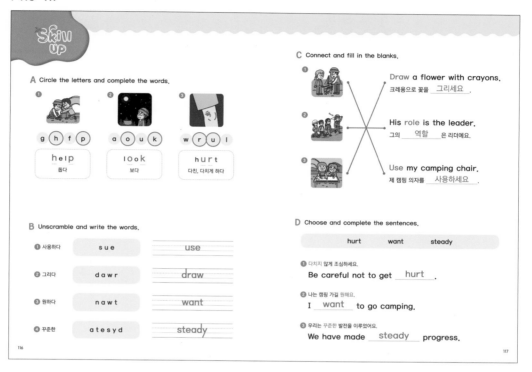

A Circle the letters and complete the words.

1. g (h) f (p) → h e l p 돕다
2. a (o) u (k) → l o o k 보다
3. w (r) (u) l → h u r t 다친, 다치게 하다

B Unscramble and write the words.

1. 사용하다   s u e → use
2. 그리다   d a w r → draw
3. 원하다   n a w t → want
4. 꾸준한   a t e s y d → steady

C Connect and fill in the blanks.

1. Draw a flower with crayons.
   크레용으로 꽃을 <u>그리세요</u>.
2. His role is the leader.
   그의 <u>역할</u>은 리더예요.
3. Use my camping chair.
   제 캠핑 의자를 <u>사용하세요</u>.

D Choose and complete the sentences.

hurt   want   steady

1. 다치지 않게 조심하세요.
   Be careful not to get <u>hurt</u>.
2. 나는 캠핑 가길 원해요.
   I <u>want</u> to go camping.
3. 우리는 꾸준한 발전을 이루었어요.
   We have made <u>steady</u> progress.

116   117

P119

 Pop Quiz [✓] 돈 [ ] 가게   [✓] 낭비하다 [ ] 믿다

P122~123

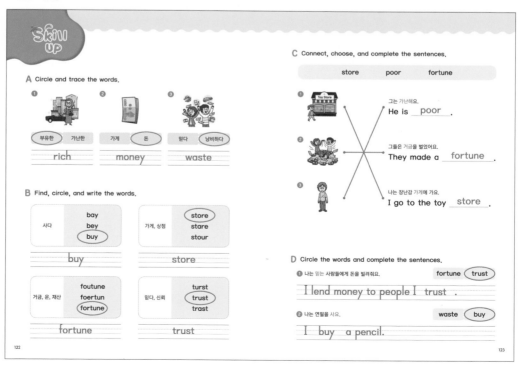

A Circle and trace the words.

1. (부유한) 가난한 → rich
2. 가게 (돈) → money
3. 믿다 (낭비하다) → waste

B Find, circle, and write the words.

사다   bay / bey / (buy) → buy

가게, 상점   (store) / stare / stour → store

거금, 운, 재산   foutune / foertun / (fortune) → fortune

믿다, 신뢰   turst / (trust) / trast → trust

C Connect, choose, and complete the sentences.

store   poor   fortune

1. 그는 가난해요.
   He is <u>poor</u>.
2. 그들은 거금을 벌었어요.
   They made a <u>fortune</u>.
3. 나는 장난감 가게에 가요.
   I go to the toy <u>store</u>.

D Circle the words and complete the sentences.

1. 나는 믿는 사람들에게 돈을 빌려줘요.   fortune (trust)
   I lend money to people I <u>trust</u>.
2. 나는 연필을 사요.   waste (buy)
   I <u>buy</u> a pencil.

122   123

Day 18

P125

Pop Quiz ✓ 뺨 ☐ 발 ✓ 이, 치아 ☐ 몸, 신체

P128~129

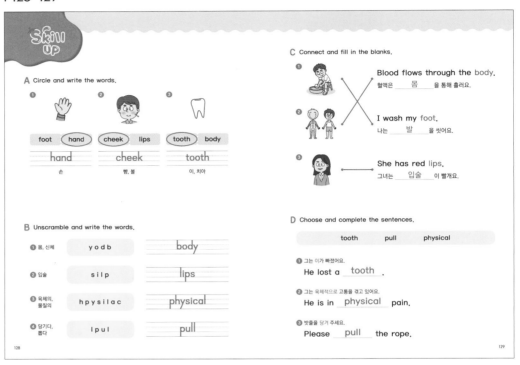

Skill Up

A Circle and write the words.

1. foot (**hand**) → hand 손
2. (**cheek**) lips → cheek 뺨, 볼
3. (**tooth**) body → tooth 이, 치아

B Unscramble and write the words.

1. 몸, 신체 — y o d b → body
2. 입술 — s i l p → lips
3. 육체의, 물질의 — h p y s i l a c → physical
4. 당기다, 뽑다 — l p u l → pull

C Connect and fill in the blanks.

1. Blood flows through the body. 혈액은 __몸__ 을 통해 흘러요.
2. I wash my foot. 나는 __발__ 을 씻어요.
3. She has red lips. 그녀는 __입술__ 이 빨개요.

D Choose and complete the sentences.

tooth   pull   physical

1. 그는 이가 빠졌어요. He lost a __tooth__ .
2. 그는 육체적으로 고통을 겪고 있어요. He is in __physical__ pain.
3. 밧줄을 당겨 주세요. Please __pull__ the rope.

128

129

Day 19

P131

Pop Quiz ✓ 축구 ☐ 농구 ☐ 인기 있는 ✓ 자랑스러운

P134~135

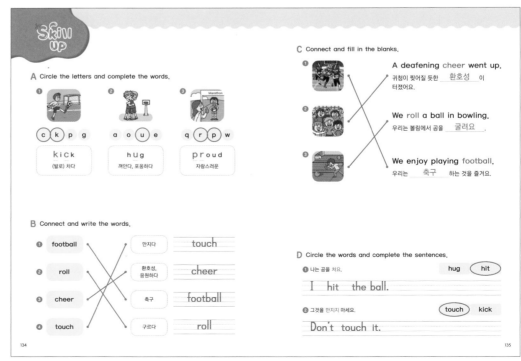

Skill Up

A Circle the letters and complete the words.

1. (**c**) (**k**) p g — k i c k (발로) 차다
2. a o (**u**) e — h u g 껴안다, 포옹하다
3. q (**r**) (**p**) w — p r o u d 자랑스러운

B Connect and write the words.

1. football — 만지다 → touch
2. roll — 환호성, 응원하다 → cheer
3. cheer — 축구 → football
4. touch — 구르다 → roll

C Connect and fill in the blanks.

1. A deafening cheer went up. 귀청이 찢어질 듯한 __환호성__ 이 터졌어요.
2. We roll a ball in bowling. 우리는 볼링에서 공을 __굴려요__ .
3. We enjoy playing football. 우리는 __축구__ 하는 것을 즐겨요.

D Circle the words and complete the sentences.

1. 나는 공을 쳐요. hug (**hit**)
   I __hit__ the ball.
2. 그것을 만지지 마세요. (**touch**) kick
   Don't touch it.

134

135

Day 20

P137

Pop Quiz ✓ 일기 ☐ 지도 ☐ 비행하다 ✓ 항해하다

P140~141

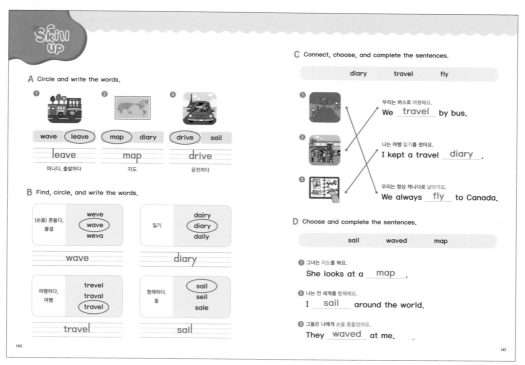

Skill UP

A Circle and write the words.

❶ wave (leave) → leave 떠나다, 출발하다
❷ (map) diary → map 지도
❸ drive sail → drive 운전하다

B Find, circle, and write the words.

(손을) 흔들다, 물결 — weve (wave) weva → wave
일기 — dairy (diary) daily → diary
여행하다, 여행 — trevel traval (travel) → travel
항해하다, 돛 — (sail) seil sale → sail

C Connect, choose, and complete the sentences.

diary   travel   fly

❶ 우리는 버스로 여행해요.
We travel by bus.
❷ 나는 여행 일기를 썼어요.
I kept a travel diary.
❸ 우리는 항상 캐나다로 날아가요.
We always fly to Canada.

D Choose and complete the sentences.

sail   waved   map

❶ 그녀는 지도를 봐요.
She looks at a map.
❷ 나는 전 세계를 항해해요.
I sail around the world.
❸ 그들은 나에게 손을 흔들었어요.
They waved at me.

140   141

Day 16~20

P142

WORD PUZZLE Complete the word puzzle. Then write the sentence.

Word Bank
look · help · trust · store · lips
pull · cheer · roll · map · wave

l o o k
c h e e r
t r u s t
l i p s
s t o r e
r o l l
m a p
w a v e
h e l p
p u l l

Let's travel!

142

P144

Review Test

맞힌 개수 : ☐ / 40

❶ use	사용하다	㉑ 돕다	help	
❷ look	보다	㉒ 원하다	want	
❸ draw	그리다	㉓ 역할, 배역	role	
❹ hurt	다친, 다치게 하다	㉔ 꾸준한	steady	
❺ money	돈	㉕ 가게, 상점	store	
❻ buy	사다	㉖ 가난한	poor	
❼ rich	부자인, 부유한	㉗ 믿다, 신뢰	trust	
❽ fortune	거금, 운, 재산	㉘ 낭비하다	waste	
❾ hand	손	㉙ 이, 치아	tooth	
❿ foot	발	㉚ 몸, 신체	body	
⓫ lips	입술	㉛ 육체의, 물질의	physical	
⓬ cheek	뺨, 볼	㉜ 당기다, 뽑다	pull	
⓭ kick	(발로) 차다	㉝ 구르다	roll	
⓮ touch	만지다	㉞ 치다, 때리다	hit	
⓯ hug	껴안다, 포옹하다	㉟ 축구	football	
⓰ cheer	환호성, 응원하다	㊱ 자랑스러운	proud	
⓱ wave	(손을) 흔들다, 물결	㊲ 지도	map	
⓲ fly	날다, 비행하다	㊳ 여행하다, 여행	travel	
⓳ leave	떠나다, 출발하다	㊴ 일기	diary	
⓴ sail	항해하다, 돛	㊵ 운전하다	drive	

144

Day 21

P147

Pop Quiz 　□ 개미　☑ 개구리　☑ 독　□ 구름

P150~151

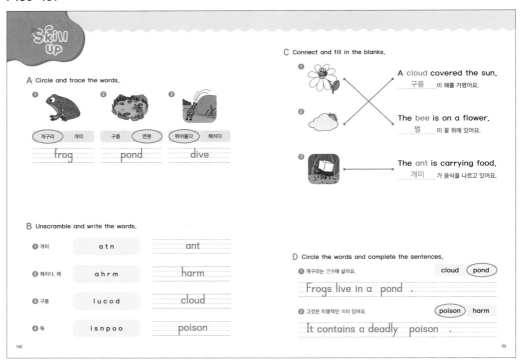

Skill Up

A Circle and trace the words.

1. 개구리 / 개미 — frog
2. 구름 / 연못 — pond
3. 뛰어들다 / 해치다 — dive

B Unscramble and write the words.

1. 개미 　a t n　 ant
2. 해치다, 해　a h r m　 harm
3. 구름　l u c o d　 cloud
4. 독　i s n p o o　 poison

C Connect and fill in the blanks.

1. A cloud covered the sun.
   구름 이 해를 가렸어요.
2. The bee is on a flower.
   벌 이 꽃 위에 있어요.
3. The ant is carrying food.
   개미 가 음식을 나르고 있어요.

D Circle the words and complete the sentences.

1. 개구리는 연못에 살아요.　cloud / pond
   Frogs live in a pond .
2. 그것은 치명적인 독이 있어요.　poison / harm
   It contains a deadly poison .

150　　151

Day 22

P153

Pop Quiz 　□ 눈이 오다　☑ 비가 오다　☑ 축축한　□ 빛나는

P156~157

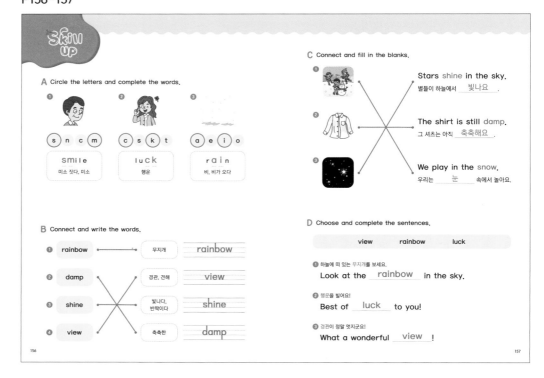

Skill Up

A Circle the letters and complete the words.

1. s n c m — smile 미소 짓다, 미소
2. c s k t — luck 행운
3. a e i o — rain 비, 비가 오다

B Connect and write the words.

1. rainbow — 무지개 — rainbow
2. damp — 경관, 견해 — view
3. shine — 빛나다, 반짝이다 — shine
4. view — 축축한 — damp

C Connect and fill in the blanks.

1. Stars shine in the sky.
   별들이 하늘에서 빛나요 .
2. The shirt is still damp.
   그 셔츠는 아직 축축해요 .
3. We play in the snow.
   우리는 눈 속에서 놀아요 .

D Choose and complete the sentences.

　view　　rainbow　　luck

1. 하늘에 떠 있는 무지개를 보세요.
   Look at the rainbow in the sky.
2. 행운을 빌어요!
   Best of luck to you!
3. 경관이 정말 멋지군요!
   What a wonderful view !

156　　157

Day 23

 **Pop Quiz** ☐ 해안 ✓ 사막 ☐ 추운 ✓ 따뜻한

P162~163

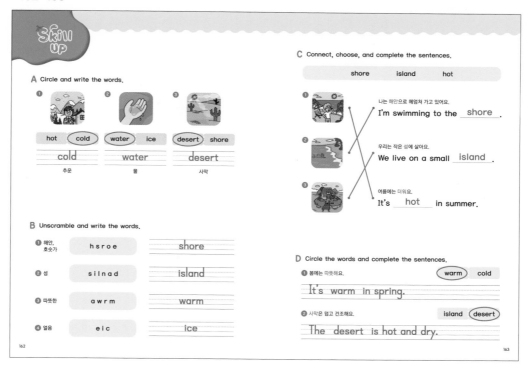

A Circle and write the words.

① (cold) — cold 추운
② (water) — water 물
③ (desert) — desert 사막

B Unscramble and write the words.

① 해안, 호숫가 h s r o e — shore
② 섬 s i l n a d — island
③ 따뜻한 a w r m — warm
④ 얼음 e i c — ice

C Connect, choose, and complete the sentences.

shore   island   hot

① 나는 해안으로 헤엄쳐 가고 있어요.
I'm swimming to the shore .

② 우리는 작은 섬에 살아요.
We live on a small island .

③ 여름에는 더워요.
It's hot in summer.

D Circle the words and complete the sentences.

① 봄에는 따뜻해요. (warm) cold
It's warm in spring.

② 사막은 덥고 건조해요. island (desert)
The desert is hot and dry.

Day 24

 **Pop Quiz** ✓ 입다 ☐ 읽다 ✓ 단순한, 간단한 ☐ 따뜻한

P168~169

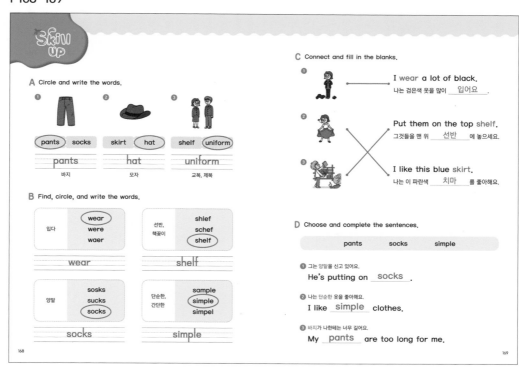

A Circle and write the words.

① (pants) — pants 바지
② (hat) — hat 모자
③ (uniform) — uniform 교복, 제복

B Find, circle, and write the words.

입다 (wear) / were / waer — wear
선반, 책꽂이 shlef / schef / (shelf) — shelf
양말 sosks / sucks / (socks) — socks
단순한, 간단한 sample / (simple) / simpel — simple

C Connect and fill in the blanks.

① I wear a lot of black.
나는 검은색 옷을 많이 입어요

② Put them on the top shelf.
그것들을 맨 위 선반 에 놓으세요.

③ I like this blue skirt.
나는 이 파란색 치마 를 좋아해요.

D Choose and complete the sentences.

pants   socks   simple

① 그는 양말을 신고 있어요.
He's putting on socks .

② 나는 단순한 옷을 좋아해요.
I like simple clothes.

③ 바지가 나한테는 너무 길어요.
My pants are too long for me.

Day 25

P171

Pop Quiz ☐ 천사 ✓ 공포 ✓ 유령 ☐ 벌레

P174~175

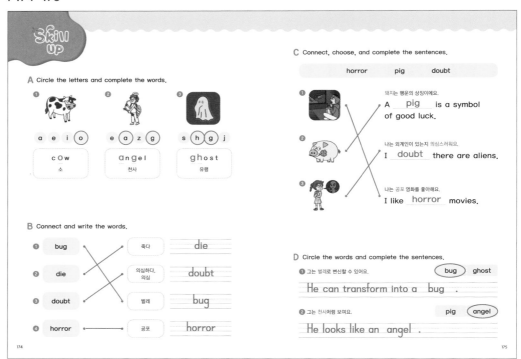

Skill UP

A Circle the letters and complete the words.

1. (o) c O w 소
2. (a)(g) a n g e l 천사
3. (h)(g) g h o s t 유령

B Connect and write the words.

1. bug — 죽다 → die
2. die — 의심하다, 의심 → doubt
3. doubt — 벌레 → bug
4. horror — 공포 → horror

C Connect, choose, and complete the sentences.

horror   pig   doubt

1. 돼지는 행운의 상징이에요.
   A _pig_ is a symbol of good luck.
2. 나는 외계인이 있는지 의심스러워요.
   I _doubt_ there are aliens.
3. 나는 공포 영화를 좋아해요.
   I like _horror_ movies.

D Circle the words and complete the sentences.

1. 그는 벌레로 변신할 수 있어요. (bug) ghost
   He can transform into a _bug_ .
2. 그는 천사처럼 보여요. pig (angel)
   He looks like an _angel_ .

174   175

Day 20~25

P176   P178

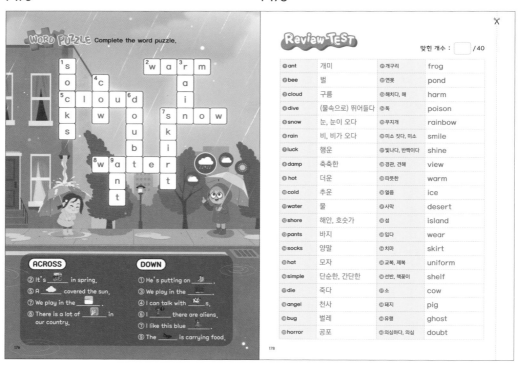

WORD PUZZLE Complete the word puzzle.

ACROSS
2. It's ___ in spring.
5. A ___ covered the sun.
7. We play in the ___.
8. There is a lot of ___ in our country.

DOWN
1. He's putting on ___.
3. We play in the ___.
4. I can talk with ___s.
6. I ___ there are aliens.
7. I like this blue ___.
9. The ___ is carrying food.

Review TEST

맞힌 개수 : ___ / 40

❶ ant	개미		㉑ 개구리	frog	
❷ bee	벌		㉒ 연못	pond	
❸ cloud	구름		㉓ 해치다, 해	harm	
❹ dive	(물속으로) 뛰어들다		㉔ 독	poison	
❺ snow	눈, 눈이 오다		㉕ 무지개	rainbow	
❻ rain	비, 비가 오다		㉖ 미소 짓다, 미소	smile	
❼ luck	행운		㉗ 빛나다, 반짝이다	shine	
❽ damp	축축한		㉘ 경관, 견해	view	
❾ hot	더운		㉙ 따뜻한	warm	
❿ cold	추운		㉚ 얼음	ice	
⓫ water	물		㉛ 사막	desert	
⓬ shore	해안, 호숫가		㉜ 섬	island	
⓭ pants	바지		㉝ 입다	wear	
⓮ socks	양말		㉞ 치마	skirt	
⓯ hat	모자		㉟ 교복, 제복	uniform	
⓰ simple	단순한, 간단한		㊱ 선반, 책꽂이	shelf	
⓱ die	죽다		㊲ 소	cow	
⓲ angel	천사		㊳ 돼지	pig	
⓳ bug	벌레		㊴ 유령	ghost	
⓴ horror	공포		㊵ 의심하다, 의심	doubt	

176   178

Word List

a
admire	존경하다
airplane	비행기
angel	천사
ant	개미
apple	사과

b
ball	공
balloon	풍선
bank	은행
basket	바구니
bat	방망이, 배트
bee	벌
bell	초인종, 종
boat	보트, (작은) 배
body	몸, 신체
boil	끓이다, 끓다
book	책
brave	용감한
brown	갈색(의)
bug	벌레
burn	타다, 화상을 입다
burst	터뜨리다, 터지다
buy	사다

c
canvas	캔버스 천
car	자동차
carrot	당근
catch	잡다
cheek	뺨, 볼
cheer	환호성, 응원하다
classroom	교실
clock	시계
cloud	구름
cold	추운
corner	모퉁이
cow	소
cut	자르다, 베다

d
damage	피해, 훼손하다
damp	축축한
desert	사막
destroy	파괴하다
diary	일기
die	죽다
dish	접시, 요리
dive	(물속으로) 뛰어들다
doubt	의심하다, 의심
draw	그리다
drink	마시다
drive	운전하다

e
eat	먹다

f
fall	떨어지다
fan	선풍기, 부채
farm	농장
fear	공포, 두려움
float	뜨다
fly	날다, 비행하다
foot	발
football	축구
fortune	거금, 운, 재산
frame	액자, 틀
frog	개구리
fry	(기름에) 튀기다

g
gate	대문, 문
gentle	다정한, 온화한
ghost	유령
gift	선물
grape	포도
gray	회색(의)

h
hand	손
handle	손잡이, 다루다
harm	해치다, 해
hat	모자
have	가지다

heat
heat	열기, 열
help	돕다
hit	치다, 때리다
horror	공포
hot	더운
house	집
hug	껴안다, 포옹하다
hurt	다친, 다치게 하다

i
ice	얼음
island	섬

j
join	함께 하다, 가입하다
journal	잡지, 신문
journey	여행
joy	기쁨, 즐거움

k
kick	(발로) 차다
kind	친절한
knife	칼, 나이프
know	알다

l
lamp	램프, 등
leap	뛰다, 뛰어오르다
leave	떠나다, 출발하다
like	좋아하다
lips	입술
look	보다
luck	행운

m
make	만들다
map	지도
mix	섞다
money	돈
mood	기분
movie	영화

n

name	이름
neighbor	이웃
nice	좋은, 멋진
novel	소설

p

pack	(짐을) 싸다, 꾸러미
paint	칠하다, 그리다
pants	바지
paper	종이
park	공원
passenger	승객
pear	배
physical	육체의, 물질의
piece	한 조각
pig	돼지
pink	분홍색(의)
poem	시
poison	독
pond	연못
poor	가난한
popular	인기 있는
potato	감자
pour	붓다, 따르다
proud	자랑스러운
pull	당기다, 뽑다
put	놓다

r

rain	비, 비가 오다
rainbow	무지개
read	읽다
refrigerator	냉장고
rich	부자인, 부유한
rock	바위, 돌
role	역할, 배역
roll	구르다
rule	규칙

s

sail	항해하다, 돛
say	말하다
school	학교
scissors	가위
seek	찾다, 구하다
select	고르다, 선택하다
sense	감각
separate	분리하다, 분리된
shape	모양
share	나누다, 공유하다
shelf	선반, 책꽂이
shine	빛나다, 반짝이다
ship	(큰) 배, 선박
shore	해안, 호숫가
show	보여 주다, 공연
silly	어리석은, 바보 같은
similar	비슷한
simple	단순한, 간단한
skip	생략하다, 건너뛰다
skirt	치마
sleep	자다
smile	미소 짓다, 미소
snow	눈, 눈이 오다
socks	양말
spoon	숟가락
squeeze	짜내다, 압착하다
steady	꾸준한
store	가게, 상점
stream	개울, 시내
student	학생
study	공부하다
subway	지하철
sure	확신하는

t

task	일, 과제
taste	맛이 ~하다, 맛
teach	가르치다
teacher	선생님
think	생각하다
tooth	이, 치아
touch	만지다
toy	장난감
train	기차
travel	여행하다, 여행
trouble	문제, 골칫거리
trust	믿다, 신뢰

u

umbrella	우산
uniform	교복, 제복
use	사용하다

v

view	경관, 견해
village	마을, 촌락
visit	방문하다

w

want	원하다
warm	따뜻한
warn	경고하다, 주의를 주다
waste	낭비하다
watch	보다
water	물
wave	(손을) 흔들다, 물결
wear	입다
white	흰색(의)
whole	전체의
wise	현명한, 지혜로운
worry	걱정하다
write	쓰다